SharePoint 2007

Tips, tricks and techniques

Working with SharePoint 2007

Saifullah Shafiq

Sadia Younas

SharePoint 2007 Tips, tricks, and techniques

Working with SharePoint 2007

Published by Lulu.com

ISBN: 978-0-557-25089-9

I dedicate this book to my parents, Dr. Shafiq Ahmed and Rashida Malik.
-Saifullah Shafiq

About the Authors

SAIFULLAH SHAFIQ is a SharePoint consultant. He started working with SharePoint technologies 6 years ago. He started his career as a web developer 11 years ago. His community work started with the start of his career. He started writing programming articles in 1999. His work has been published on 62 programming related web sites. He has also written for different IT magazines.

Saifullah is a MCP (C#), MCTS (SharePoint) and MVP (SharePoint). Saifullah runs a SharePoint usergroup that has over 450 members.

SADIA YOUNAS is an experienced IT professional. Sadia loves writing about SharePoint and has enormous experience in setting up SharePoint across enterprises.

Table of Contents

Introduction

This is not the first book on SharePoint 2007 and definitely not the last one. Several books have been written about this excellent product but each was unique in its own way and provided useful insight into different product areas. This book does not focus on one particular topic, or let me put it this way, it focuses on different topics that are of interest to the real world users. It has small tips. It sheds light on some very common error messages that users get during the development. The book discusses ways to resolve these errors. Book also discusses new Office products that can be used with SharePoint 2007. You can consider it a series of articles where each article or section focuses on one particular area of the product and teaches you something new about SharePoint. SharePoint is huge product. There are different books that have been written to cover different areas of this product. Some areas that users are particularly interested in are related to web services, workflows, search, web parts and business intelligence. This book will teach you development and deployment of web services. It also shows you how custom web parts work in SharePoint and discusses their source code. There is one chapter that tells you how SharePoint search works and you can customize it. This book does not cover workflows and business intelligence. Each section in each of the chapters gives users step-by-step guide on how to develop or deploy something in SharePoint. This book will cater to the needs of average SharePoint users. All applications discussed in the book are available for download from my website.

Users will learn the following from this book:

- Installing SharePoint 2007
- Configuring SharePoint 2007
- Using Office products with SharePoint 2007
- Developing InfoPath applications
- Creating web services
- Installing web services (Creating installers)

Who this book is for

This book is for everyone but because it covers different topics, I would say it will be more beneficial to the beginners and people with intermediate level skills. Anyone using SharePoint would find something of value in this book. The book is structured in a way that all chapters are unrelated to each other. You can pick up the book, open the chapter you are interested in getting help from and start reading it. As I mentioned earlier, the book is a collection of articles that focus on particular areas of the product. This is particularly useful for the users who are just starting on learning the product because you don't have to go through the whole book to understand the topic discussed in the last chapter. My experience tells me that users (readers) are interested in step-by-step walk-throughs. They want to get to the core of the functionality that they are interested in without diving deep into it. MSDN and Technet have extensive documentation on SharePoint but still people prefer reading blogs because each blog gives them a quick solution to their problem and that's the main reason why blogs are so popular. So, this book is a cook book and contains recipes that users will find delicious and useful.

Chapter 1

Installing Microsoft Office SharePoint Server (MOSS) 2007

In this chapter:

- SharePoint Installation Pre-requisities
- SharePoint Installation
- SharePoint Configuration Wizard

SharePoint is an integrated suite of server capabilities. Running different software in different environments has always been a headache for companies. SharePoint has resolved this issue to some extent, if not completely. Now companies can manage their operations using a single software and good thing is that external applications can also be integrated into SharePoint. I always call SharePoint collaboration software. Companies can connect their departments and employees scattered in different places. Not only collaboration but SharePoint also provides excellent content management solution. SharePoint provides tools for server administration, application extensibility and interoperability. Installing SharePoint can be difficult depending on the complexity of the environment. In this chapter, we will cover only a single machine installation. A picture speaks a thousand words. This chapter uses screenshots to show you each step of the installation. This, I believe, will help users, specially the beginners to better understand each step during the installation process.

SharePoint Installation Pre-requisities

If you don't have a licensed version, you can install a trial version that can be downloaded from the following page:

http://www.microsoft.com/downloads/details.aspx?FamilyId=2E6E5A9C-EBF6-4F7F-8467-F4DE6BD6B831&displaylang=en

I would recommend that you install MOSS on a fresh machine. You can install it on a virtual machine. I have tested it both with VMware and VPC. Hardware and software requirements are listed on the following page:

http://office.microsoft.com/en-us/sharepointserver/HA101945391033.aspx

You should have at least 3 GB space free on your hard disk and at least 1 GB RAM, although 2 GB RAM is recommended for good performance. On my machine, it took approx. 2.3 GB to install SharePoint, WinFX, SQL Server and I spent approx. one and a half hour in installing all these products.

1. Install IIS 6 with ASP.NET enabled.
2. Disable Internet Enhanced Security in Internet Explorer. You can disable it by going to Add/Remove Windows components.
3. Install SQL Server. MOSS 2007 can be installed with both SQL Server 2000 and 2005. You can also install MOSS 2007 with SQL Server 2008. You can read more about it on the following page:

   http://blogs.msdn.com/sharepoint/archive/2008/08/15/sql-server-2008-support-for-sharepoint-products-and-technologies.aspx

   If you are installing SQL Server 2000 then make sure you install SQL Server 2000 Service Pack 3 as well.

TIP

If you have an old installation file that is in ISO format, you can still install it. You can download ISOBuster or any other ISO software to extract setup files from the ISO image. I would recommend WinRAR. There is a problem with other ISO software. You get "Language not supported" error during installation. The solution to "Language not supported" error is to use RAR instead of ISO software. Simply, change the extension of the downloaded file to .RAR and then use WinRAR to extract files from the ISO image.

---

4. Download WinFX from the following page:

http://www.microsoft.com/downloads/details.aspx?FamilyID=4A96661C-05FD-430C-BB52-2BA86F02F595&displaylang=en

Be careful with the version of WinFX. Versions earlier than this won't work with MOSS 2007 and will give you an error during the MOSS installation. You should not download the version older than the following one:

File Name:	winfxsetup.exe
Version:	3.0.3906.22
Date Published:	5/23/2006
Language:	English
Download Size:	2.5 MB

Run winfxsetup.exe downloaded from the location shown above. Winfxsetup.exe will download more files from the internet and it can take around 30-40 minutes for the setup to complete. This includes downloading 46 MB of data from the internet. This will install the components required for the MOSS setup.

SharePoint Installation

5. Run the SharePoint setup file to start the installation. You will be asked to enter the license key.

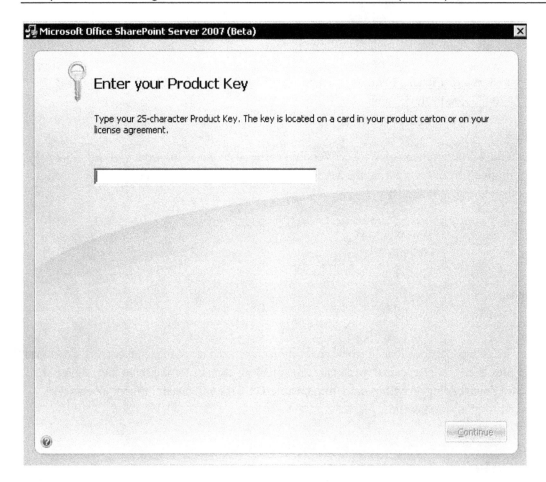

Figure 1.1: *Enter license key*

Enter your license key and click the "Continue" button.

6. Next screen, you will be asked to accept the license agreement.

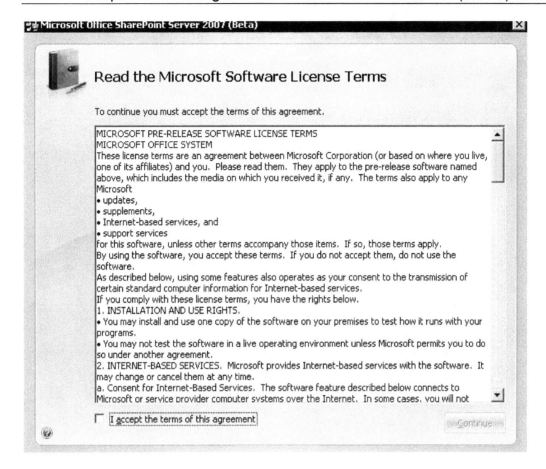

Figure 1.2: *Accept license*

Click the checkbox and "Continue" button to proceed.

7. In next screen, you will be asked to select "Basic" or "Advanced" setup. Select "Advanced".

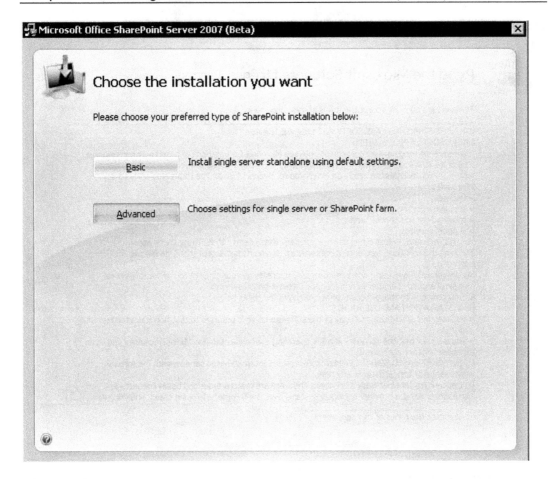

Figure 1.3: *Select installation type*

8. Select "Complete" installation type in the next screen. The other two options are:

- Web Front End
- Standalone

Click "Install Now".

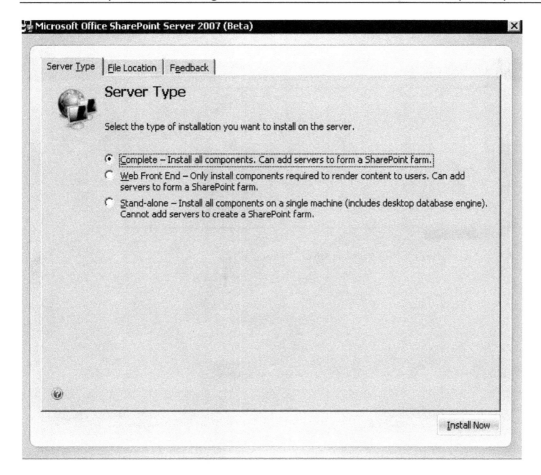

Figure 1.4: *Server Type*

9. Installation will start and you will see a blue progress bar.

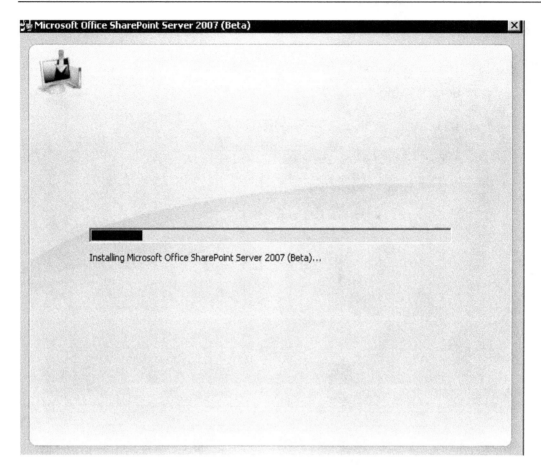

Figure 1.5: *Installation in progress*

It will take approx. 10 minutes for the installation to complete. You will see following screen when your installation is complete:

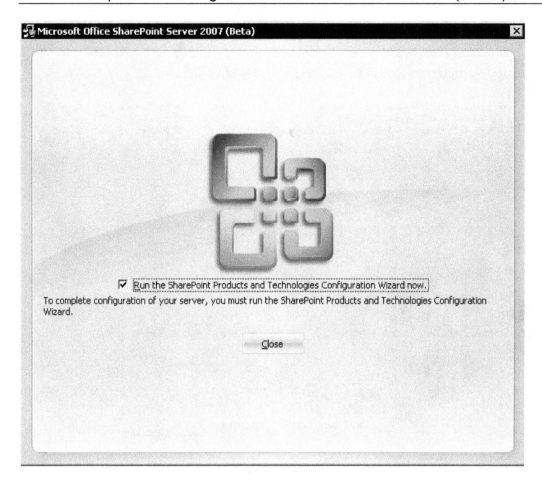

Figure 1.6: *Installation complete*

SharePoint Configuration Wizard

Now your SharePoint installation is complete and it's time to configure the application. Check the checkbox and click the "Close" button. You will see another screen:

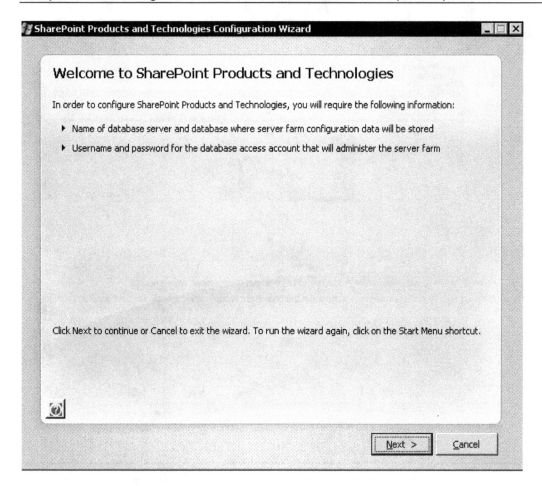

Figure 1.7: *Configure SharePoint*

Click "Next" to start the configuration process.

   10. You might see the following message when you click the "Next" button:

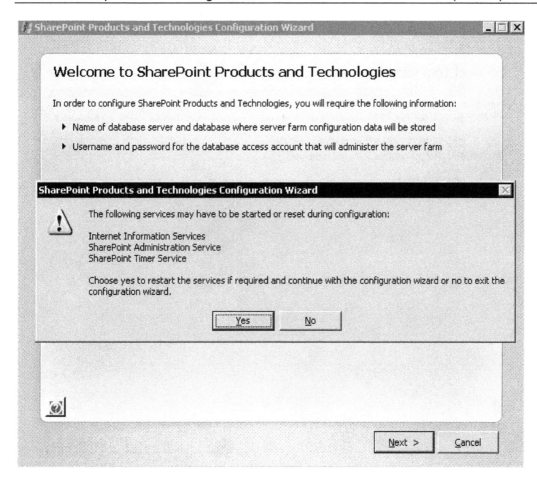

Figure 1.8: *Start services*

Click "Yes"!

11. In the next screen, you will be asked to select a server farm. Click "No" to create a new server farm and click "Next".

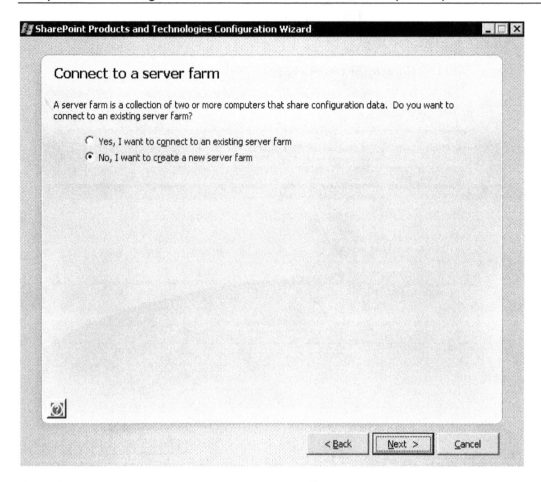

Figure 1.9: *Connect to a server farm*

12. Enter your database server and database name in the next screen which looks like this:

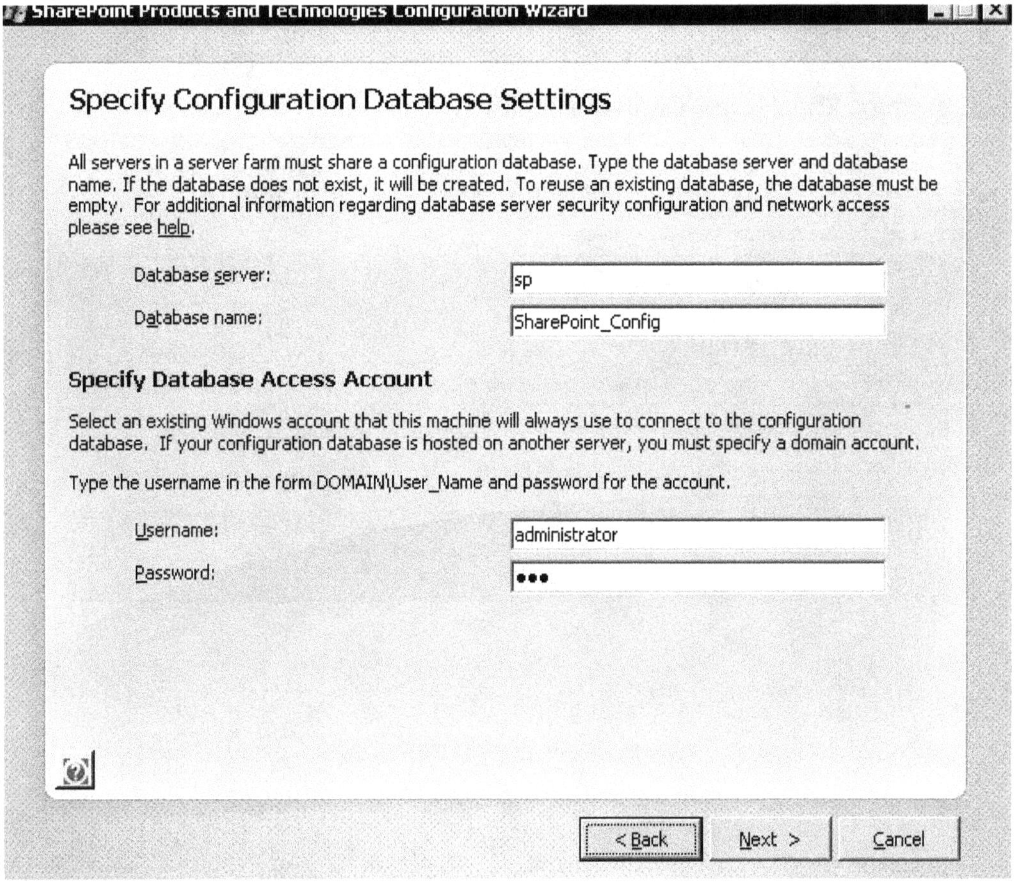

Figure 1.10: *Database settings*

Also, enter username and password that will be used to access your database. I used my local Admin account. Click "Next" to proceed.

13. Select security options. You can change the port number and security configuration in this screen:

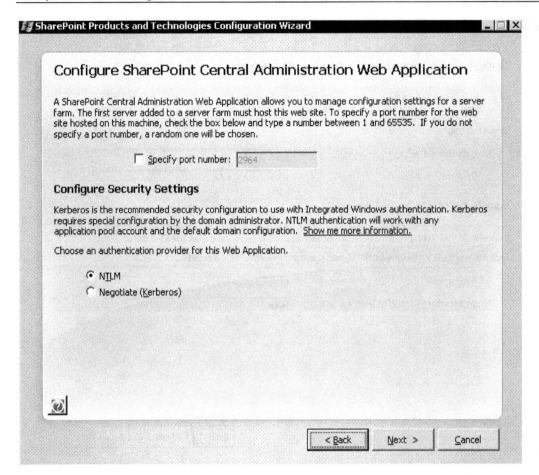

Figure 1.11: *Configure Central Administration*

Select default options and click "Next".

14. You will see the following screen:

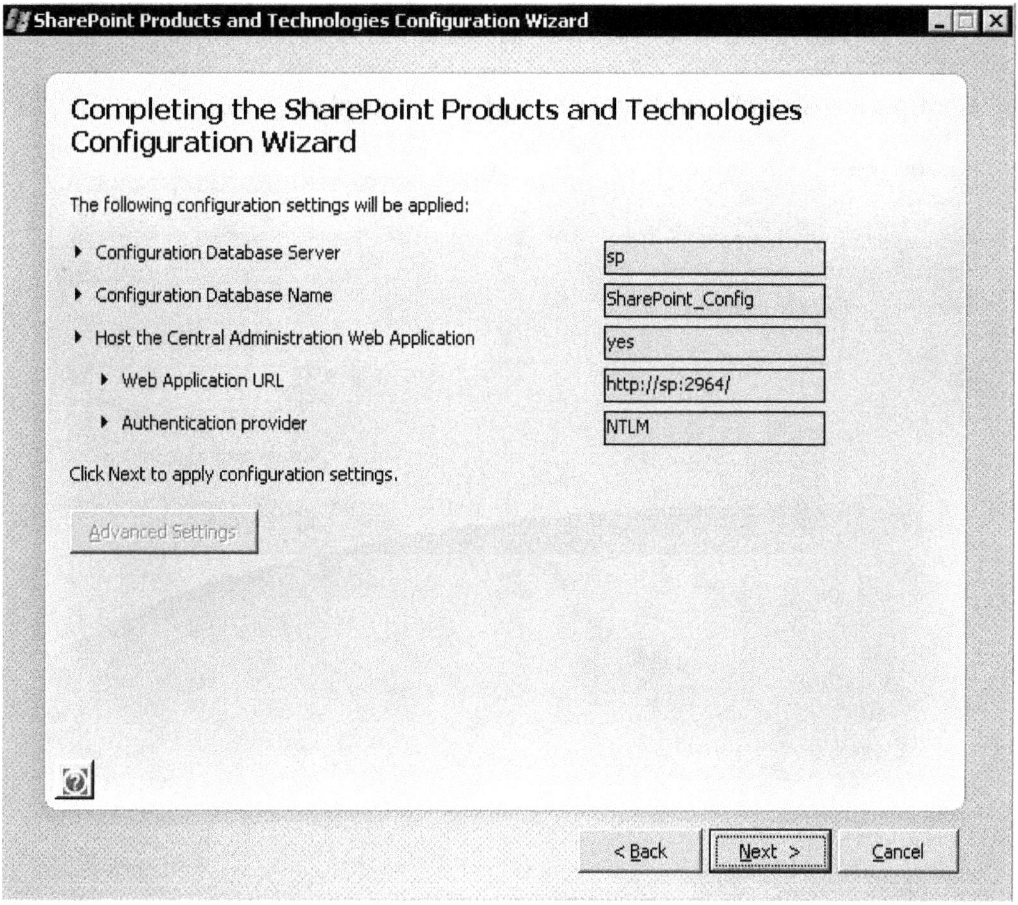

Figure 1.12: *Configuration wizard*

Click "Next" to proceed.

It will take sometime for the configuration to complete. You will see a progress bar during the configuration process:

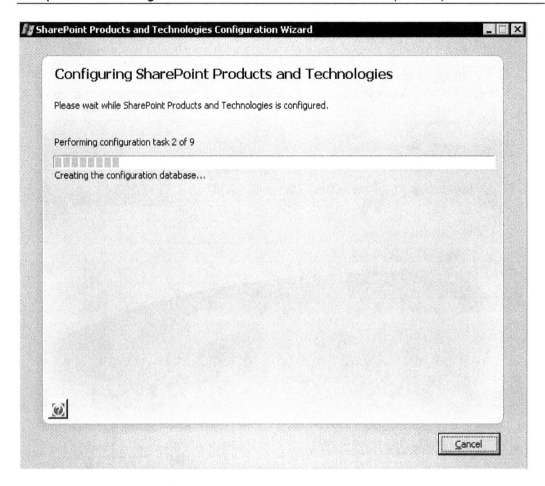

Figure 1.13: *Installation in progress*

15. Finally, you will see the "Configuration Successful" message. Click "Finish" and you are done!

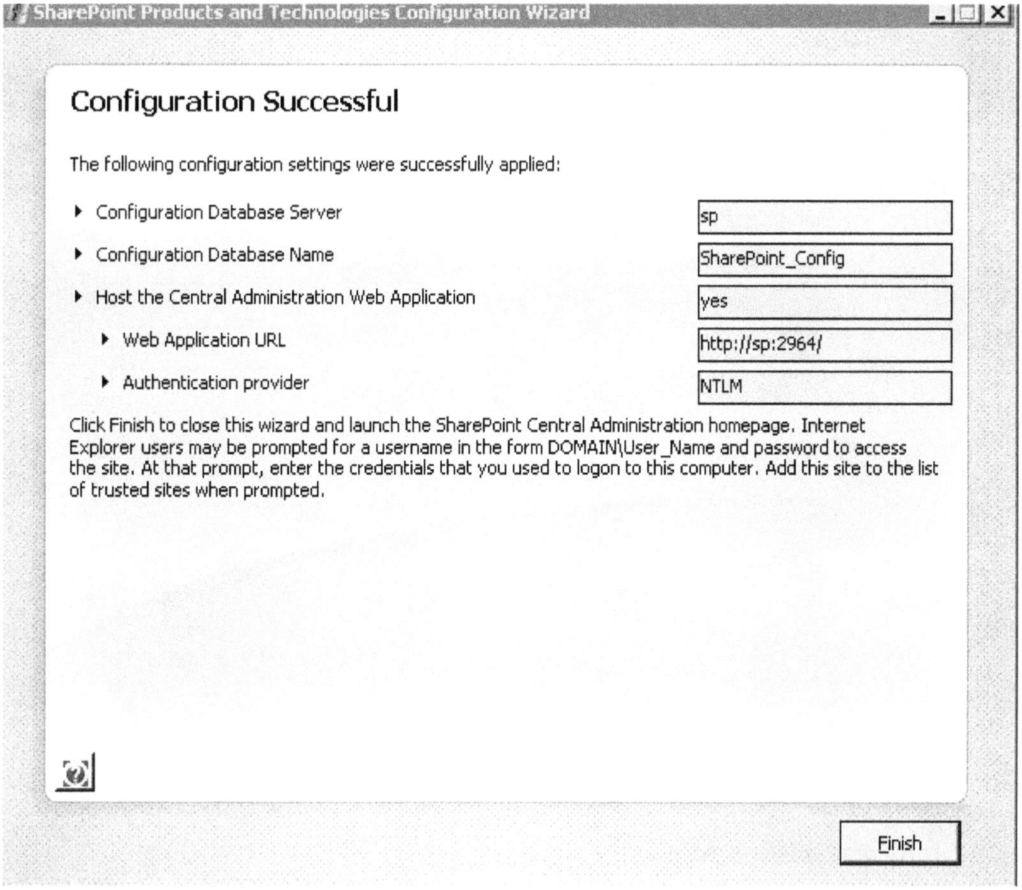

Figure 1.14: *Configuration successful*

Here is the first screen that you will see after configuration:

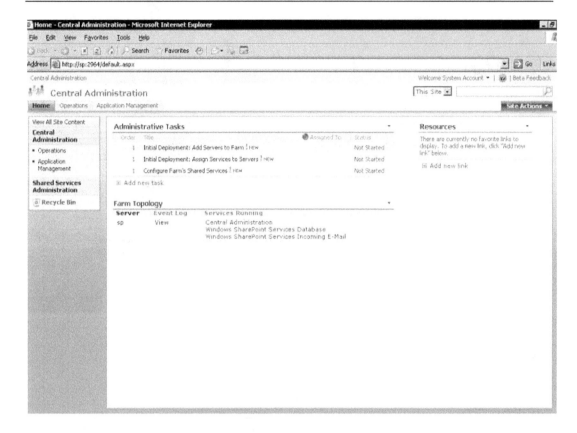

Figure 1.15: *SharePoint homepage*

Congratulations! MOSS 2007 has been setup.

Summary

This chapter introduced you to the SharePoint installation and configuration. Although it looks straight forward but first time installation and configuration is a headache, especially for the beginners. This chapter mostly relied on the screenshots which give you a clear picture of the steps involved in the installation. Chapter also showed you how to configure SharePoint and database settings using the configuration wizard.

Chapter 2

Creating a Site Collection

In this chapter:

- SharePoint Central Administration
- Manage farm's shared services
- Create or extend web application
- Create site collection

As the name suggests, site collection is a collection of sites that can be managed from a single location. All sites in a site collection have common features and navigation. A site collection has a single top level site and top level site has subsites. A subsite is a site within a site collection. A subsite can inherit settings like permissions and navigation from the parent site. This chapter gives you the steps required to create a site collection.

After the setup and configuration is complete, you will be presented with a SharePoint Central Administration screen. Your first task is to enable some important services on the server. Click on the "Operations" tab and then select "Services on server".

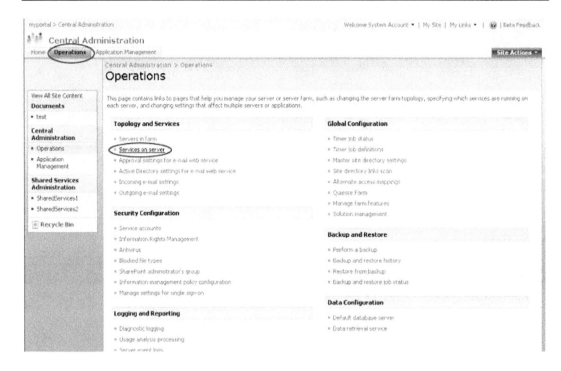

Figure 2.1: *Central administration operations*

You will see a screen similar to the following:

Figure 2.2: *Services on server*

Select "Single Server or Web Server for small server farms" if you are using a single machine for your deployment. Start the services shown in red boxes in the figure shown above. These services are: Office SharePoint Server Search and Windows SharePoint Services Web Application.

You can also create "Shared Services" for your farm. SharePoint will automatically create shared services for the site collection you will create but if you want to see how shared services are created then follow the instructions shown next.

Click on the "Application Management" tab and then click "Create or configure this farm's shared services" link (encircled in red in the figure shown below).

Figure 2.3: *Application management*

You will be presented with the following screen:

Figure 2.4: *Manage farm's shared services*

You can see in the figure above that I have already created a couple of shared services. Click on the "New SSP" link to create a new shared service, this will open a new page. Most of the fields in this page will already have been populated with default values. Enter a name in the "SSP

Name" field and select your newly created application from the "Web application" drop down. Enter your username and password in the "SSP Service Credentials".

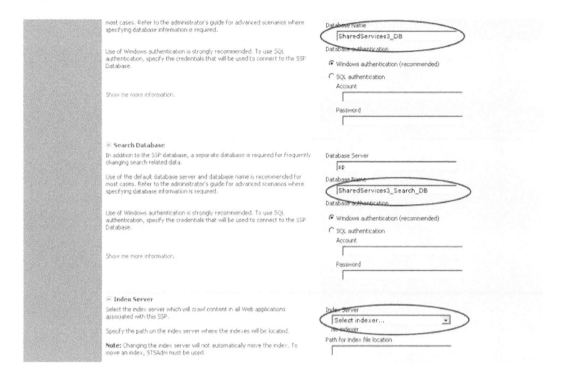

Figure 2.5: *SSP service credentials*

SharePoint will automatically add a name for the database that will be created for the shared service. You can change this name if you want. You can select a database authentication method. Windows authentication is the recommended option but you can also use SQL authentication. A search database will also be created and you will have the option to rename this database. Select authentication method for this database and finally, you will have to select an index server. In my case, it is the SQL server that hosts my SharePoint DBs. If you have a separate index server, you can choose it in the "Index Server" drop down, otherwise, choose the default SQL server and click "OK".

Now, you can start creating a web application. Select "Application Management" tab and click on "Create or extend Web application".

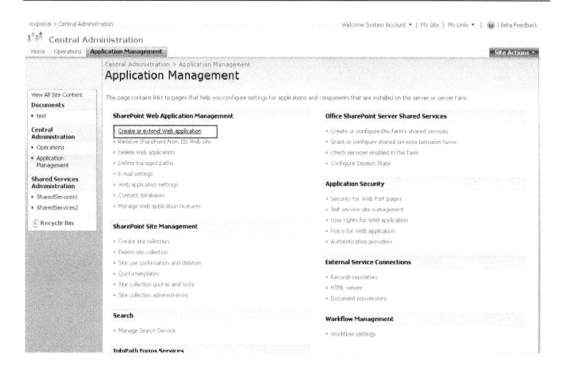

Figure 2.6: *Create or extend web application*

Select "Create a new Web Application" next.

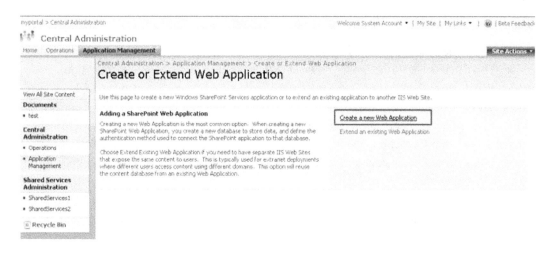

Figure 2.7: *Create a new Web Application*

In the next screen, you will set lot of properties. Start with IIS Web Site. Create a new IIS web site, enter description in the "Description" field. Select a port other than 80 if you already have an application running on port 80. Path is auto selected and you can change the destination but I would recommend the default location to be used. Have a look at the screen below. You can copy values exactly from this screen. Use your userid and password for application pool identity. Similarly, select an authentication type for database and provide security credentials. Finally, hit OK to continue.

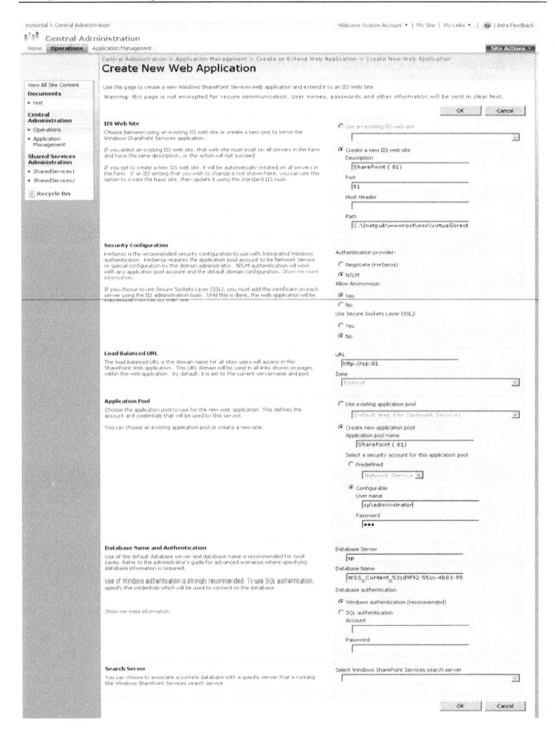

Figure 2.8: *New application settings*

Now that you have created a web site, it's time to create a top level site or site collection for your portal. You can name it as "Portal" and the URL will be http://portal if you created web site on port 80. Select "Application Management" tab and then select "Create site collection" link in "SharePoint Site Management" section.

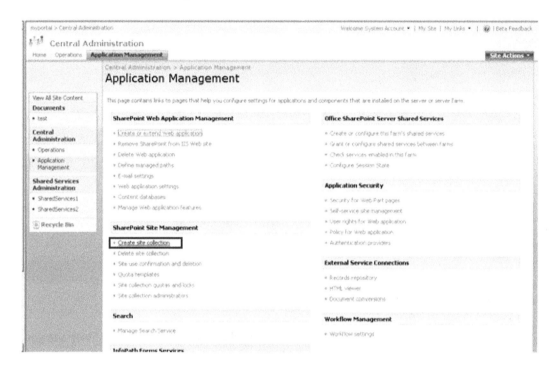

Figure 2.9: *Create site collection*

This will bring up a new page where you will have the option to select a web site. Select your newly created web application by clicking the arrow in the dropdown box.

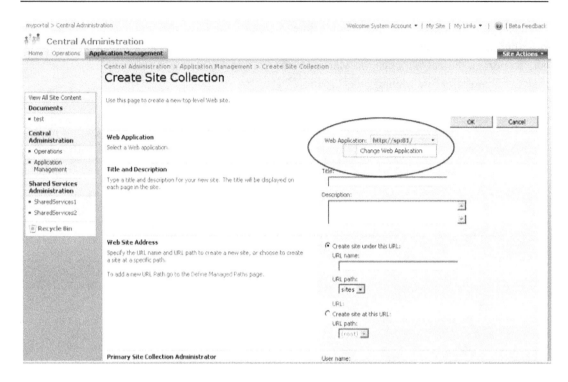

Figure 2.10: *Change web application*

Select "Create site at this URL:" option to create a site collection on the root of the web site you created. In this case, your final URL will look like:

http://portal

and if you select "Create site under this URL" then your URL will look like:

http://portal/sites/mysite.

Provide a name for primary site collection administrator. In templates, select "Corporate Intranet Site" (Click "Publishing" tab to select this template) template and click OK.

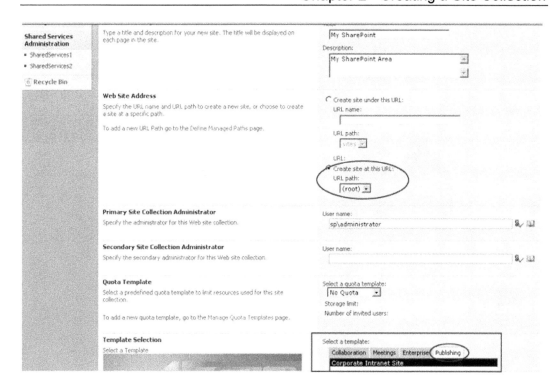

Figure 2.11: *Site url*

Here is how your portal site will look like:

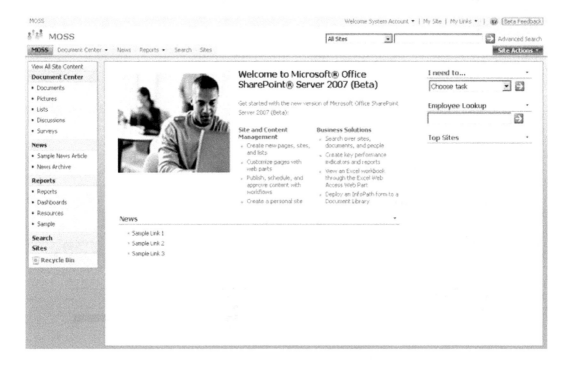

Figure 2.12: *Portal site*

Summary

This chapter gave you the exact steps required to create a site collection. It is important that these steps are followed in the order they were presented. You were introduced to SharePoint central administration and several of its key areas.

Chapter 3

SharePoint and MS Office

In this chapter:

- OneNote and SharePoint
- Groove and SharePoint
- Publishing PowerPoint slides in SharePoint
- MS Access and SharePoint

SharePoint is collaboration software and integrates very well with MS Office applications. Below I will show you how it works with other Microsoft Office products.

OneNote and SharePoint

You can read more about Microsoft Office OneNote 2007 on Microsoft site:

http://office.microsoft.com/en-us/onenote/default.aspx

You can read more about SharePoint Server 2007 on Microsoft site:

http://office.microsoft.com/en-us/sharepointserver/FX100492001033.aspx

It will not be wrong to call OneNote an e-notebook. In OneNote, one can write down notes of all kind and share them with others easily. Users can easily manipulate information in OneNote. They can add, delete, edit information without any problem and good thing is they can share this information with others. There are different ways of sharing this information with people. Email used to be a popular method of sharing information but with the increase in the popularity of

SharePoint, more and more people are turning toward the OneNote-SharePoint combination. There are some very good blogs that discuss OneNote in detail:

Chris Pratley's OneNote Blog: http://blogs.msdn.com/chris_pratley/
Owen Braun's OneNote Blog: http://blogs.msdn.com/owen_braun
Donovan Lange's OneNote Blog: http://blogs.msdn.com/dolange
Daniel Escapa's OneNote Blog: http://blogs.msdn.com/descapa

In this chapter, I will explore some sharing features of OneNote and see how SharePoint is used to share notes from OneNote.

Live Sharing

1. In the menu bar, select Share > Live Sharing Session > Start Sharing Current Section.

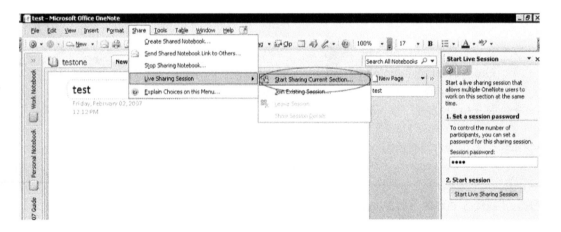

Figure 3.1: *Live sharing*

2. In the "Start Live Session" task pane, enter a session password and click Start Live Sharing Session button.

3. In the "Current Live Session" task pane, you will find following three options:

a. Go to Live Shared Section
b. Invite Participants
c. Leave Live Sharing Session

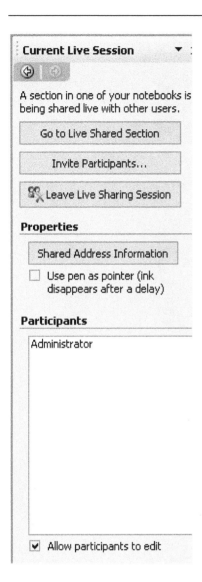

Figure 3.2: *Live session*

4. Click Invite Participants to invite more people to this live session. Clicking the Invite Participants button will open an email editor. Insert users in the To: field and click Send.

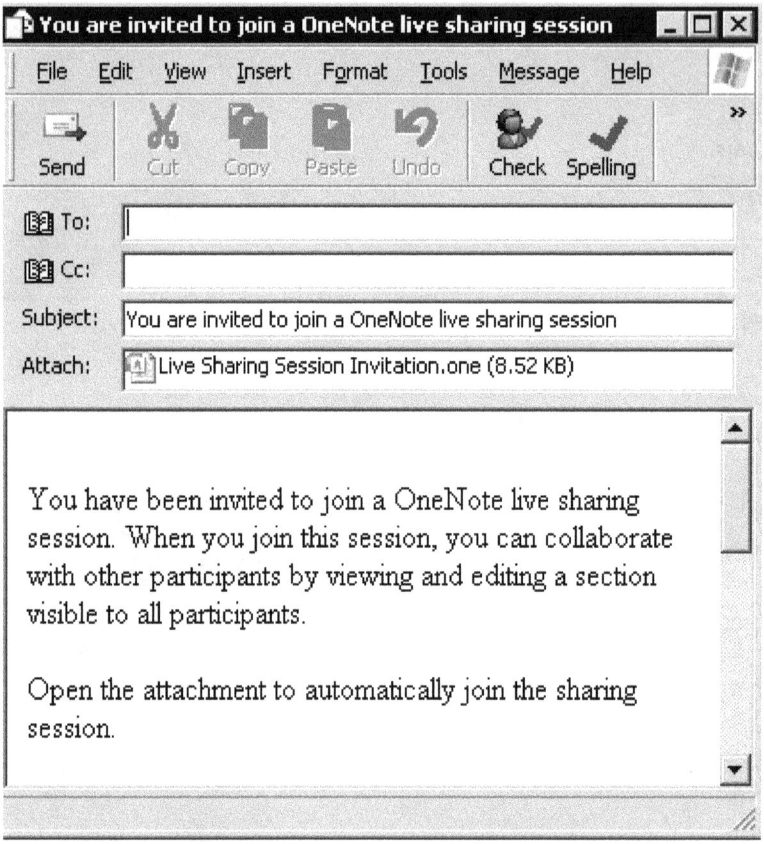

Figure 3.3: *OneNote live sharing session invitation*

Shared Notebook

Ok, time to see SharePoint in action!

1. In the menu bar, select Share > Create Shared Notebook...

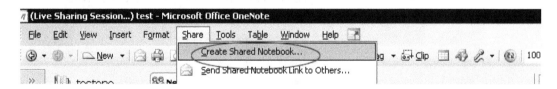

Figure 3.4: *Shared Notebook*

2. Enter a name for your shared notebook in the Name field and select a color of your choice. There are different templates available for you to select. I selected Shared Notebook - Reference Materials. Click Next to proceed.

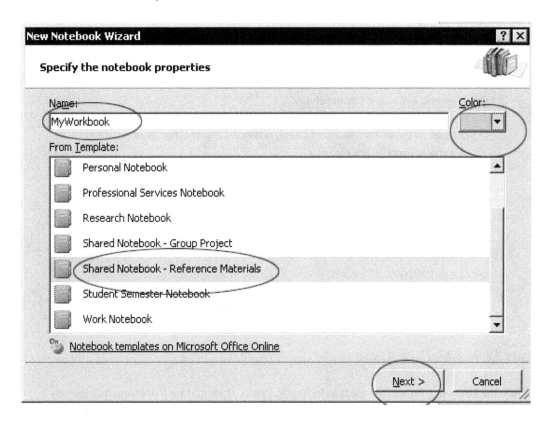

Figure 3.5: *Notebook properties*

3. Select the third option Multiple people will share the notebook and select On a server ... in the other options.

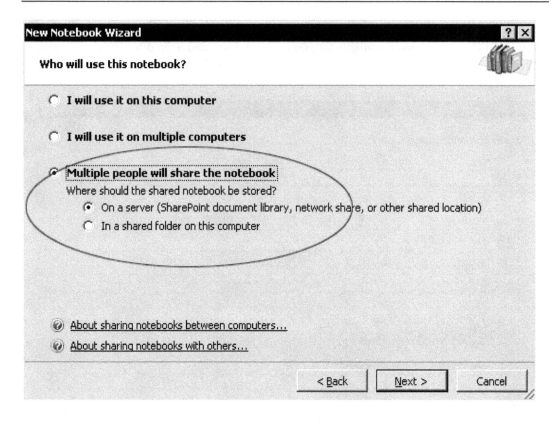

Figure 3.6: *New Notebook Wizard*

4. Click the Browse... button to select a destination path. It should be a document library in SharePoint. Check the checkbox shown at the bottom if you want to create an email to send to other people and finally, click Create.

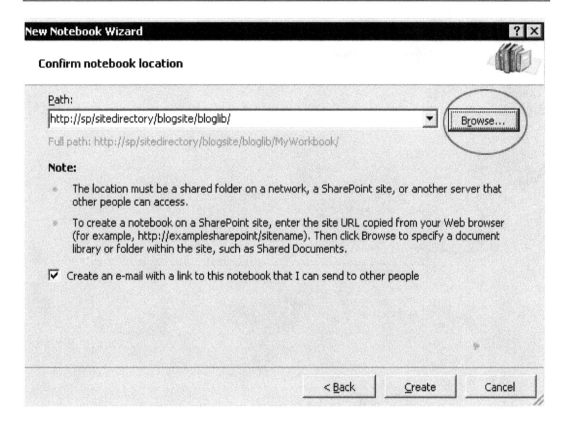

Figure 3.7: *Notebook location*

5. This will create a shared notebook in SharePoint. Now, to test sharing, create a note and type something in it and select File > Save As from the menu bar.

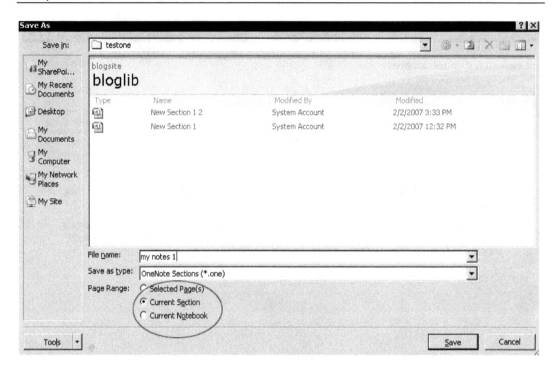

Figure 3.8: *Save notebook*

6. Enter a file name and select a page range. You have following options to save the note book:

a. Selected Pages.
b. Current Section
c. Current Notebook.

Select an option and click the Save button. This will save your note in SharePoint. If you open SharePoint, you will see your note saved in there. Click the link to the saved note in SharePoint and it will open the note in OneNote. Now, everyone in the document library will have access to the note. You can manage permissions in the document library. Contributors will be able to modify your saved notebook.

7. You can manage SharePoint document library right from within OneNote. Select Tools > Document Management from the menu bar.

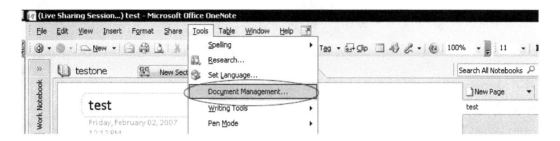

Figure 3.9: *Document management*

8. This will open Document Management task pane on the right.

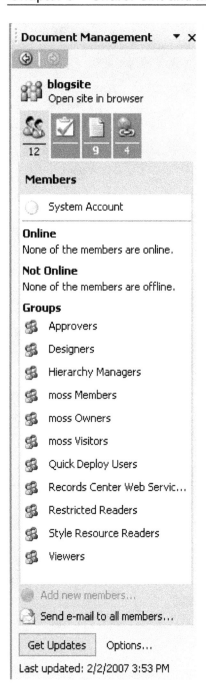

Figure 3.10: *Document management*

The first icon shows the members of the document library and number below the icon is the total number of members in the document library. The second icon shows the tasks. The third icon shows the number of items in the library and the number below the icons shows the number of items. The fourth option shows the links. Move mouse over one of the listed links, a drop down will appear, open it. You will see three options. You can edit the listed link or even delete it permanently and if you want to be notified about the changes in this link, select the third option. It will take you to the alerts setting page in SharePoint where you will be able to subscribe to the alert.

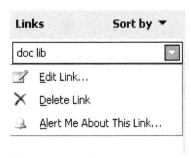

Figure 3.11: *Links*

That's it.

There are a couple of nice tips on Olya's blog (http://blogs.msdn.com/olya_veselova/):

1. Assigning Outlook tasks from OneNote shared notebooks (http://blogs.msdn.com/olya_veselova/archive/2006/10/05/Assigning-Outlook-tasks-from-OneNote-shared-notebooks.aspx)

2. Enabling searching of OneNote content on SharePoint sites: (http://blogs.msdn.com/olya_veselova/archive/2006/09/25/770917.aspx)

Groove and SharePoint

Let's explore how Groove works in conjunction with SharePoint. To learn more about Groove 2007, visit following link:

http://office.microsoft.com/en-us/groove/HA101656331033.aspx

Groove is a collaboration software that helps teams work together in an effective manner. Users can work online or offline and anywhere they like. There are a number of pre-built tools available in Groove that can help users in increasing their productivity. Following tools are available in Groove:

1. Calendar
2. Chess Game
3. Custom
4. Discussion
5. Files
6. Forms
7. InfoPath Forms
8. Issue Tracking
9. Meetings
10. Notepad
11. Pictures
12. SharePoint Files
13. Sketchpad

With all these tools, working and collaborating on projects has become extremely easy. You don't have to worry about the whereabouts of your team members. Every one can contribute to the project. In this walk through, we will cover "SharePoint Files" tool and see how Groove works with SharePoint.

1. If you have Groove properly installed and configured, you will be asked to log in before accessing Groove's services.

Figure 3.12: *Groove login screen*

2. You see notifications after logging in. Notifications window show any files pending for synchronization.

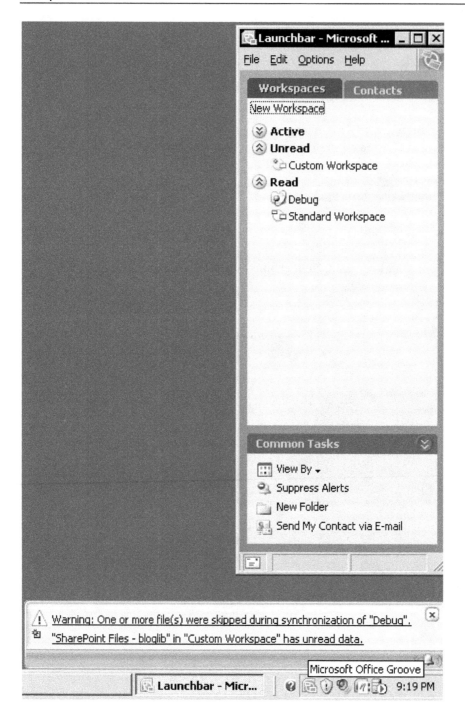

Figure 3.13: *Launch bar*

3. To create a new shared workspace, select File > New > Workspace.

Figure 3.14: *Create new workspace*

4. Enter a name for your workspace and select Standard as workspace type.

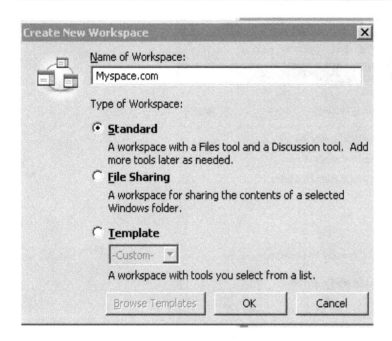

Figure 3.15: *Name new workspace*

5. Click your newly created workspace from Active workspaces if it's not visible.

Figure 3.16: *Active workspaces*

6. Click Add Tools from "Common Tasks" to add SharePoint Files tool.

Figure 3.17: *Workspace members*

7. Select SharePoint Files from the list and click OK.

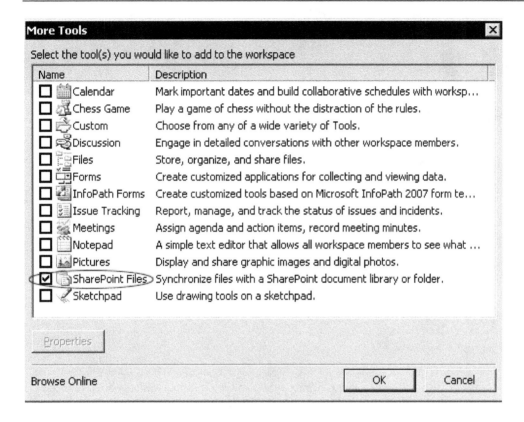

Figure 3.18: *Groove tools*

8. Following screen with a setup button will open. Click the Setup button to select the SharePoint library.

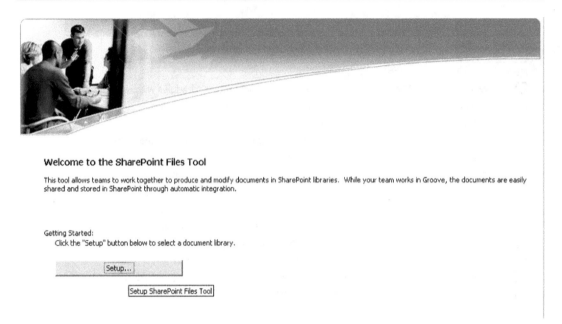

Welcome to the SharePoint Files Tool

This tool allows teams to work together to produce and modify documents in SharePoint libraries. While your team works in Groove, the documents are easily shared and stored in SharePoint through automatic integration.

Getting Started:
Click the "Setup" button below to select a document library.

Setup...

Setup SharePoint Files Tool

Figure 3.19: *SharePoint Files Tool*

9. If you know the URL of the document library, you can type it in the Address box. You can search for the SharePoint libraries from the options available on the left side. You must have appropriate permissions in SharePoint in order to browse these sites and libraries in this interface. Select a library from a list of available libraries in the site you selected and click the Select button. Clicking the Select button without selecting the library will give you an error.

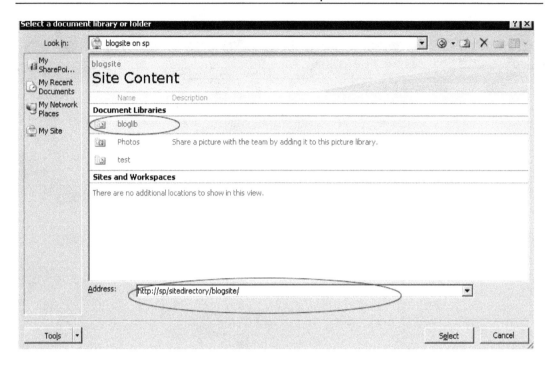

Figure 3.20: *Select SharePoint library*

10. Documents from the SharePoint library will appear in Groove. Groove will take care of the synchronization.

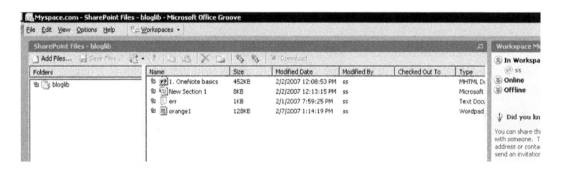

Figure 3.21: *See SharePoint files in Groove*

Let's see how Groove synchronizes files. Click Add Files... button to add a file in Groove. Select a file from the system and click the Open button. The uploaded file will immediately appear on the right side.

11. Click the Synchronize Now... button to sync the files.

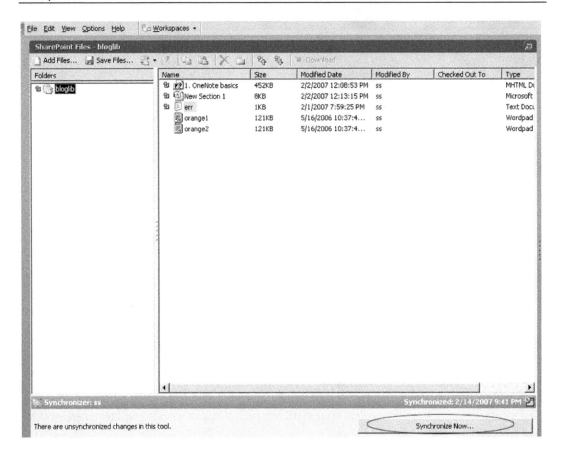

Figure 3.22: *Synchronize SharePoint files*

12. Preview Synchronization screen will show you all the pending files that need to be synchronized. Click on the file to see the summary of changes in the box below. Click Synchronize Now button to start synchronizing the files.

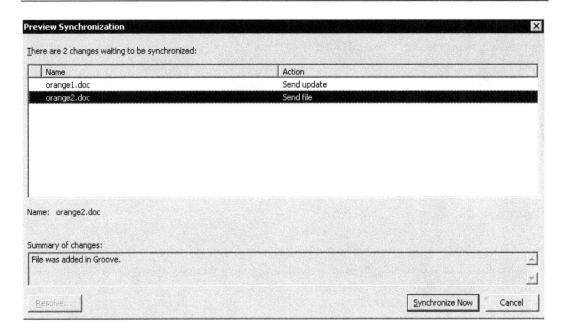

Figure 3.23: *Preview synchronization*

13. Go to your SharePoint library to see if the files have been synchronized. You will notice that new files appear with a "new" icon.

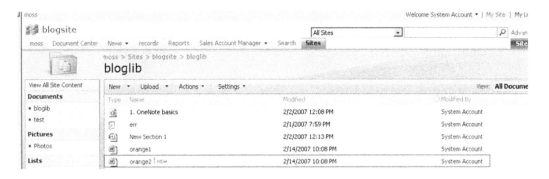

Figure 3.24: *View documents in SharePoint*

14. Now, add a file in SharePoint library and go back to the Groove application and click the Synchronize Now button. The Preview Synchronization window will show you the new file that was added in the SharePoint library with "Get File" message in the "Action" column. Click the Synchronize Now button and the file will be added to the Groove.

15. You can also check out files from SharePoint libraries. There is a button (Manage files checked out from SharePoint) in the toolbar. Click it to view the options it has. Select a file first

53

and then click Check Out from SharePoint to check out the file and your username will immediately appear in the "Checked Out To" column.

Figure 3.25: *Check Out from SharePoint*

16. There are other option available as well. For example, you can save the files in Groove to other locations like your system or other shared folders on your network which shows how useful Groove is for sharing and collaborating.

More Features

1. Click View Workspace Properties in the "Common Tasks" to see the properties of the workspace you created in Groove. There are four tabs:

- General
- Alerts
- Roles
- Permissions

There are three roles available in Groove:

- Manager
- Participant
- Guest

There are five types of permissions in Groove:

- Invite
- Uninvite
- Add Tool
- Delete Tool
- Cancel all outstanding invitations

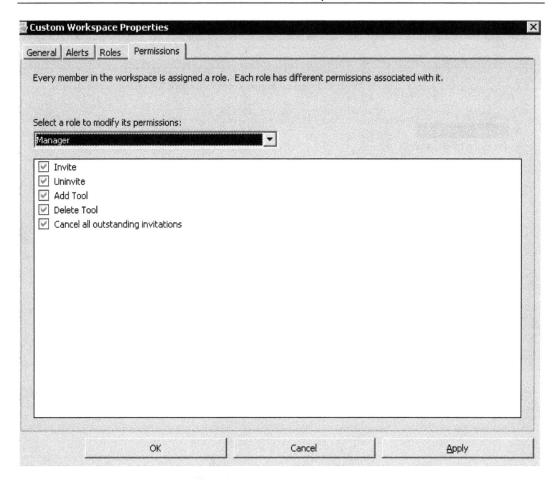

Figure 3.26: *Roles*

2. You can add other computers to your Groove network and invite users to join your workspace in Groove.

3. You can chat online with other users in your network.

4. You can send messages to other users.

5. You can also view system and presence information.

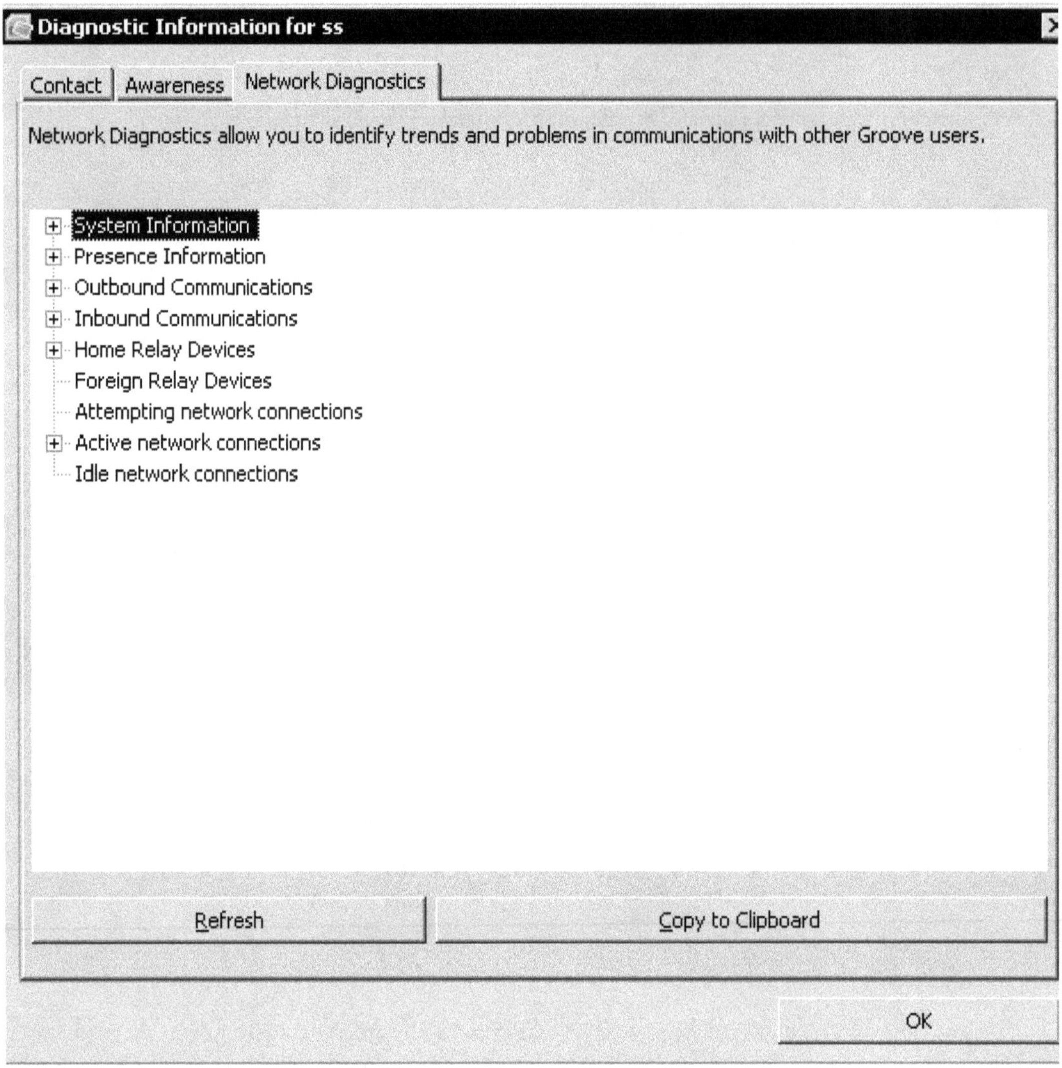

Figure 3.27: *System Information*

Publishing PowerPoint slides in SharePoint

Here is what you will learn in this topic:

1. Publishing PowerPoint files in SharePoint.
2. Synchronizing files.
3. Working with properties (Adding new properties to the PowerPoint files)
4. Publishing PPT file properties in SharePoint.
5. Searching PPT files in SharePoint.
6. Customizing SharePoint search to find PPT files using the keywords.

Like all other Office products, PowerPoint has great publishing feature and you can publish PPT slides directly to SharePoint.

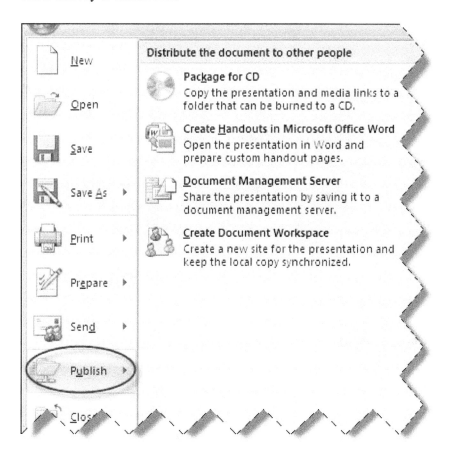

Figure 3.28: *Publishing PowerPoint slides*

As you can see in the figure above, PowerPoint shows two options to save files in SharePoint:

1. Document Management Server
2. Create Document Workspace

Create Document Workspace will allow you to create a site in SharePoint and **Document Management Server** will allow you to select a network share that points to a SharePoint site.

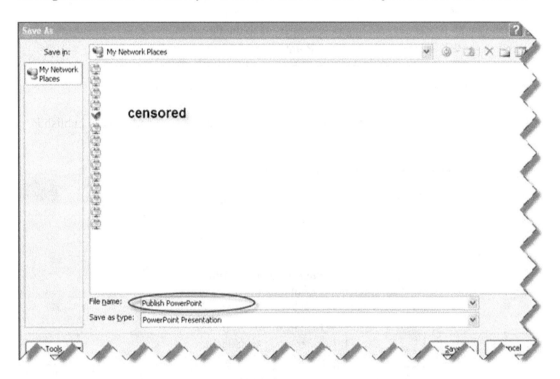

Figure 3.29: *Save PowerPoint Presentation in network places*

You can put the SharePoint site path directly in the **File name** box if you know it and PowerPoint will save the file in SharePoint.

Document Management Pane on the right shows important information related to the file.

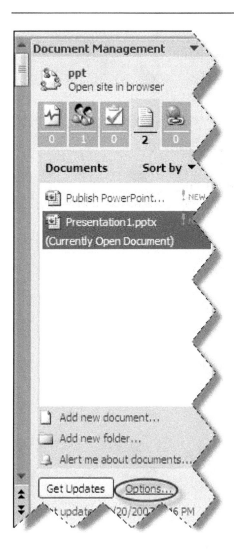

Figure 3.30: *Document Management*

To show Document Management pane, select **Server > Document Management Information**.

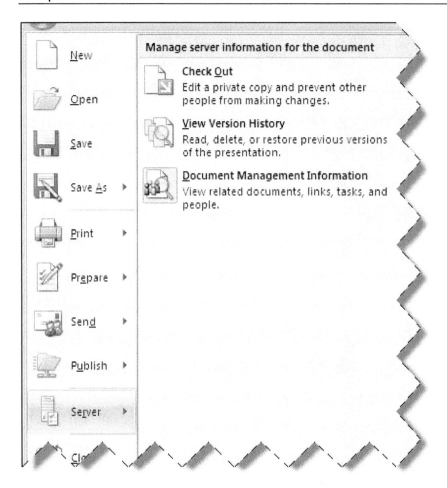

Figure 3.31: *Server options*

Click the **options** link at the bottom of the **Document Management** pane to open the settings screen.

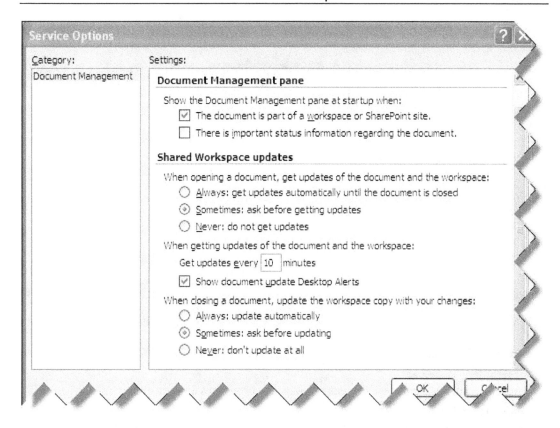

Figure 3.32: *Service Options*

You can change some important settings here. For example, to keep your local copy synchronized with the SharePoint copy select **Always: update automatically** in the last option. This will automatically update your remote copy without asking you first.

Interestingly, you can also view version history of the saved files. To view version history, select **Server > View Version History**. To view versions saved in SharePoint, click the link shown in the window.

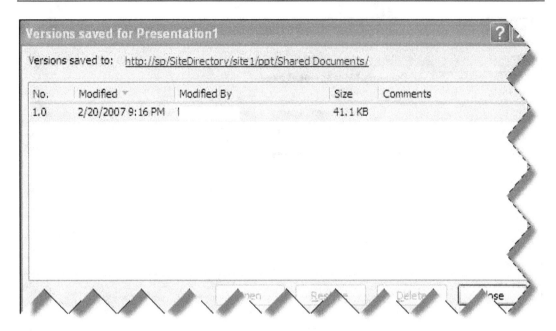

Figure 3.33: *Versions saved for a presentation*

Another very interesting and useful feature is to save properties along with the file in SharePoint. We could do this in Office 2003 as well but in Office 2007, it is now possible to view or add properties from inside the PowerPoint. Select **Prepare > Properties** from the Office button.

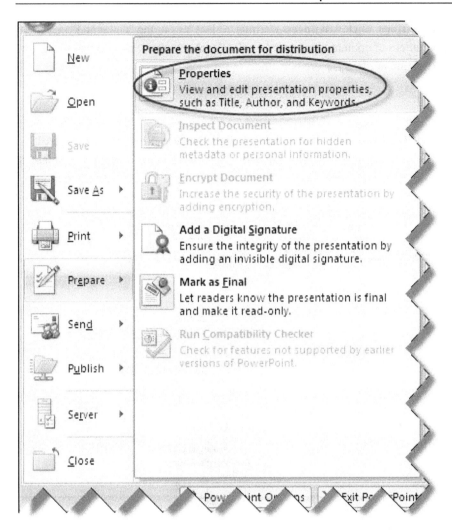

Figure 3.34: *Properties menu*

This will start showing the properties window.

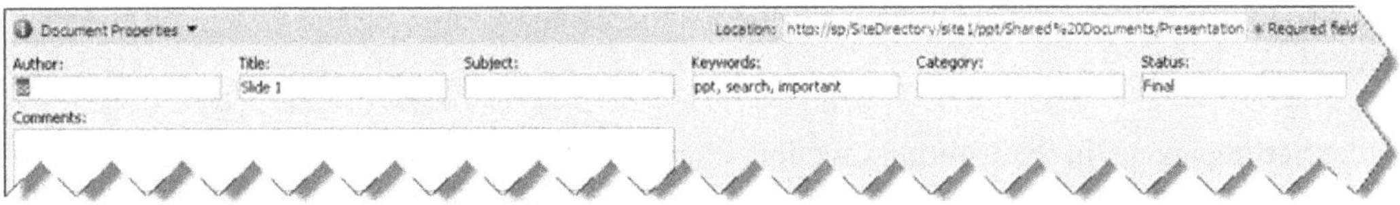

Figure 3.35: *Document properties*

Add some keywords in the **keywords** box to test this feature and save the file. Now go to your SharePoint site and open the document library. From **Settings**, select **Document Library**

63

Settings. In **General Settings**, click **Advanced settings**. Select **Yes** in the "Content Types" section (Allow management of content types?) and click **OK**. Now, there are two ways to show the properties in the document library. Here is method 1:

Method 1:

On the **Settings** page, in the **Content Types** section, click the **Document** content type. Scroll down and click **Add from existing site or site columns**. From the columns drop down, select **All Groups** (See figure below) and select **keywords** from the list and click the **Add >** button and then click **OK**.

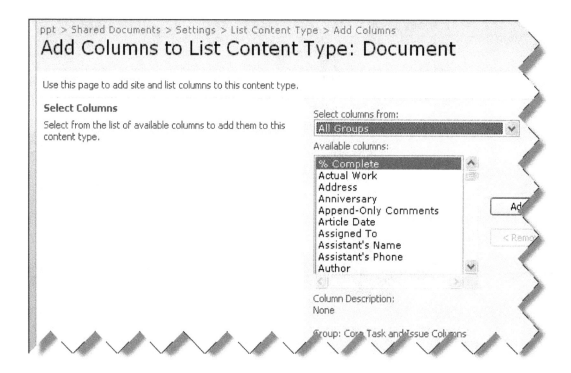

Figure 3.36: *Add columns to List Content Type*

Method 2:

On the **Settings** page, in the **Columns** section, click **Add from existing site columns**. From the "site columns" drop down, select **All Groups** and from "Available site columns" box, select keywords and click the **Add >** button to add the column to the view and click the **OK** button. Make sure **Add to default view** check box is checked at the bottom. You will notice that the new column "keyword" has been added to the list of columns available in the current view and if you look at the third column "Used in", you will see "Document" has been added as the content type.

Column (click to edit)	Type	Used in
Category	Single line of text	Document
HiddenDate	Single line of text	
Keywords	Multiple lines of text	Document
Title	Single line of text	Document
Created By	Person or Group	
Modified By	Person or Group	
~ecked ~ To	~son or ~up	

Figure 3.37: *Columns used in Document content type*

Now go back to your library and you will see the keywords you entered while working in PowerPoint have been saved in SharePoint. Similarly, you can add other fields from PowerPoint as site columns in SharePoint. If you have enabled Search for your library, you can search documents using the keywords. To enable Search, do the following:

1. Go to the **Settings** page and click on **Advanced settings** and select **Yes** in the Search section (Allow items from this document library to appear in search results?).

2. Click **OK** to save the changes.

Note: The documents will not appear in search results unless SharePoint indexes all new documents. This can be done manually from the SharePoint Central Administration.

If the documents have been indexed, you will have no difficulty in finding the documents using the site search box. As you may know, you can also search documents using keywords, which in this case are document properties, using the Advanced search. Click the **Advanced Search** link that appears next to the search box.

Advanced Search

Find documents with...

All of these words:

The exact **phrase**:

Any of these words:

None of these words:

Narrow the search...

Only the **language(s)**: ☐ French

☐ German

☐ Japanese

☐ Spanish

Result **type** All Results ▾

Add property restrictions...

Where the Property... (Pick Property) ▾ Contains ▾ And ▾ Add Property...

Figure 3.38: *Advanced Search*

Here you can use a property or a combination of properties to search files in SharePoint. Open the **Property** (Pick Property) drop down, you will notice that the site column "Keywords" that we added to our document library is not visible in this drop down by default. No problem! We can add it ourselves! Yes! this is the beauty of SharePoint. We can customize things easily in this version of the SharePoint. To add "Keywords" column to the "Property" drop down, do the following:

1. Make sure you are on the **Advanced Search** page. Now, from the **Site Actions**, select **Edit Page**.

2. Click the **edit** link and select **Modify Shared Web Part**.

Advanced Search Box edit ▾

Find documents with...

All of these words:

Figure 3.39: *Advanced Search Box*

3. In the **Advanced Search Box**, expand **Properties** by clicking the + sign.

Figure 3.40: *Advanced Search Box – Properties*

4. Click anywhere in the **Properties** box, a blue shaded "square" button (ellipsis) will appear. Click this button to view the content of the **Properties** box in an editor. You will see that the editor contains lot of text and there are quite a few sections in the code. We need to add the "Keywords" property to some of these sections in order to make it appear in the advanced search box properties.

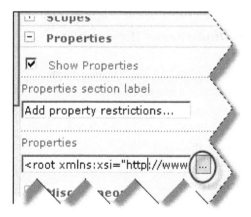

Figure 3.41: *Click ellipsis (square button with dots)*

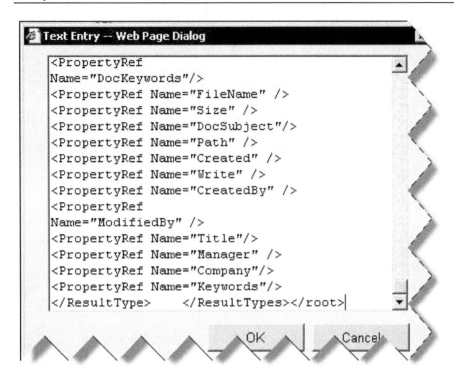

```
Text Entry -- Web Page Dialog

<PropertyRef
Name="DocKeywords"/>
<PropertyRef Name="FileName" />
<PropertyRef Name="Size" />
<PropertyRef Name="DocSubject"/>
<PropertyRef Name="Path" />
<PropertyRef Name="Created" />
<PropertyRef Name="Write" />
<PropertyRef Name="CreatedBy" />
<PropertyRef
Name="ModifiedBy" />
<PropertyRef Name="Title"/>
<PropertyRef Name="Manager" />
<PropertyRef Name="Company"/>
<PropertyRef Name="Keywords"/>
</ResultType>    </ResultTypes></root>

            OK          Cancel
```

Figure 3.42: *View content of properties box in editor*

5. Locate the **<PropertyDefs>** tag in the text and add the following property definition tag inside **<PropertyDefs>** and **</PropertyDefs>** tags.

<PropertyDef Name="Keywords" DataType="text" DisplayName="Keywords"/>

There is another property definition (docKeywords) in this section that has a display name "Keywords" so you may want to change your display name to something else, for example, "Keywords2" or "Tags". I kept the name as "Keywords" and everything worked fine.

6. Locate the tag **<ResultTypes>**. There is another tag inside this tag:

<ResultType DisplayName="All Results" Name="default">

Add the following property reference tag just before the **</ResultType>** tag:

<PropertyRef Name="Keywords" />

There are different types of results, for example, Document results, Excel results, PowerPoint results, etc. Now, because we, at the moment, are only concerned with the PowerPoint documents, therefore, we will make a change in the results of the type "PowerPoint".

7. Locate the following tag:

<ResultType DisplayName="Presentations" Name="presentations">

and add following tag just before the **</ResultType>** tag:

<PropertyRef Name="Keywords"/>

8. Click **OK** to close the editor.

9. Click **Apply** and then **OK** to save the web part changes.

10. Click the **Publish** button to save your changes.

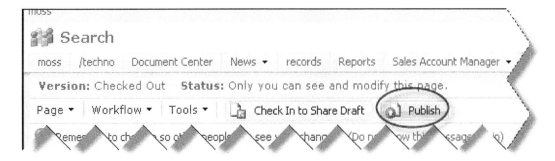

Figure 3.43: *Publish changes*

11. Now, go to the **Advanced Search** Page and search your documents using the **keywords**.

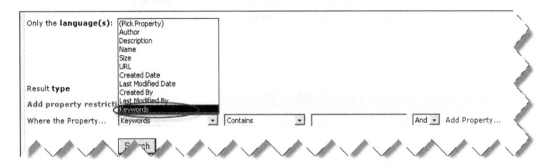

Figure 3.44: *Advanced Search*

All you have to do now is enter some relevant keywords every time you save your PowerPoint slide, PPT will be saved along with the keywords to the SharePoint library. Save as many files as you like and "SharePoint Search" will do the main job, that is, finding files for you.

MS Access and SharePoint

This section will show you how you can export data from Access to SharePoint and then import data from a SharePoint list into InfoPath. Let me tell you that you can also create an InfoPath form that could access data in an external database including Access. Using a built-in wizard in InfoPath, creating such a form is very easy. You can display data from Access in the InfoPath form. You can also incorporate search feature with ease using the wizard. This section is divided into parts. The first part shows how to export data to SharePoint from an Access database.

Export data from Access to a SharePoint list

1. Export Access data to a SharePoint list. Go to 'External Data' in Access and select 'SharePoint List' from the 'Export' section.

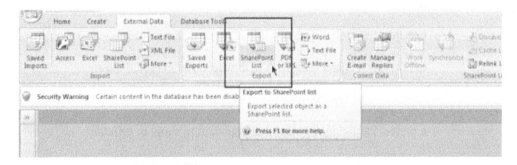

Figure 3.45: *Export to SharePoint*

Well, that's the only step required. Using the wizard you can either select a pre-built SharePoint list or you can create a new one before exporting data.

Importing data from a SharePoint list into an InfoPath Form

1. Create a new data connection in InfoPath and select following options:

   a. Create a new connection > Receive data

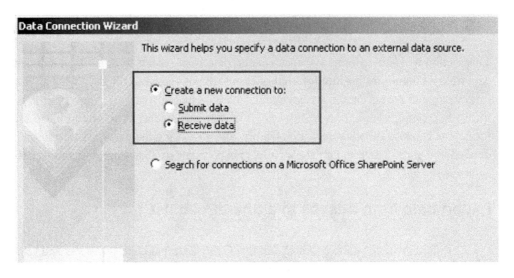

Figure 3.46: *Receive data connection*

    b. Select "SharePoint library or list" option.

    c. Enter the (SharePoint) list's path where you exported the Access data.

    d. Select your list from the list of lists and libraries.

    e. Select the field (or fields) that you want to show in InfoPath.

    f. Check 'Store a copy of the data in the form template'.

    g. Add a name for the data connection and check the "Automatically retrieve data when form is opened" option.

    h. Click "Finish".

Use following steps to populate a text box with data imported from MS Access:

    1. Add a text box in your form.

    2. Right click the text box and select "Text Box Properties" to open the properties page. Enter a default value for this field (Click the button (fx) shown on the right side of the "value" text box).

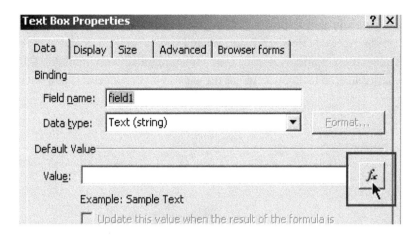

Figure 3.47: *Select a text box value*

3. Click 'Insert Field or Group...' button.

4. Select secondary data source from the 'Data source' drop down.

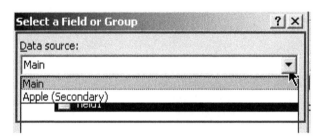

Figure 3.48: *Select main data source*

5. Expand all nodes until you see field names. Select the field that you want to retrieve value from.

6. Click OK twice and that's it!

You can use more fields to display data from different columns of the Access table.

Summary

In this chapter, you learned about different Office products and their working with SharePoint. You explored OneNote and its integration with SharePoint. Similarly, you were introduced to Groove and were shown how you could take advantage of using it with SharePoint. You saw different exciting features of Groove. You also explored publishing of PowerPoint slides in SharePoint. The chapter introduced you to the techniques for making PowerPoint slides searchable in SharePoint. You also learned about the integration of one of the most commonly used Microsoft products, Access with SharePoint. When I say integration, that doesn't mean you have to do the integration explicitly. Office is already integrated with SharePoint. It's just the features and benefits and the techniques to use these two great products together that I talk about in this chapter.

Chapter 4

Working with SharePoint

In this chapter:

- Excel Services Settings
- Anonymous access in SharePoint surveys
- Microsoft GroupBoard Workspace
- Sales Account Manager
- Displaying library items for a specific time period
- MOSS 2007 and Code Access Security

Excel Services Settings

Excel services have to be setup properly in SharePoint Central Administration before they are used in SharePoint. New users often forget to set these settings in central administration and they get permissions errors when they try to publish a report in SharePoint or try to access an Excel sheet. For example, one of the errors users get is:

You do not have permissions to open this file on Excel Services.
Make sure that the file is in an Excel Services trusted location and that you have access to the file.

Another error related to Excel Services Settings is:

The file you selected could not be found. Check the spelling of the file name and verify that the location is correct. Make sure that the file has not been renamed, moved, or deleted, that the file is in an Excel Services Trusted Location, and that you have access to the file. If the problem persists, contact your administrator.

Here is how you configure Excel Services in SharePoint Central Administration:

1. Click SSP in SharePoint Central Administration.

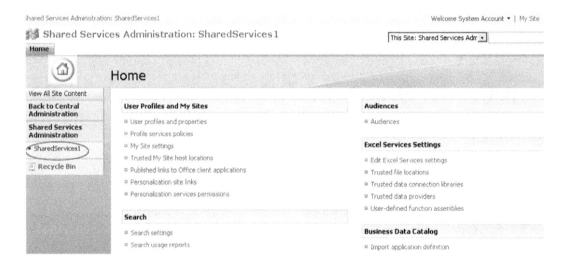

Figure 4.1: *Shared Services*

2. Click **Edit Excel Services settings** in "Excel Services Settings" section.

Figure 4.2: *Excel Services settings*

3. Select **Process account** in "File Access Method".

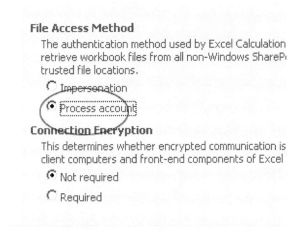

Figure 4.3: *File Access Method*

Scroll down to "External Data" section and enter user's information who has appropriate permissions in SharePoint sites.

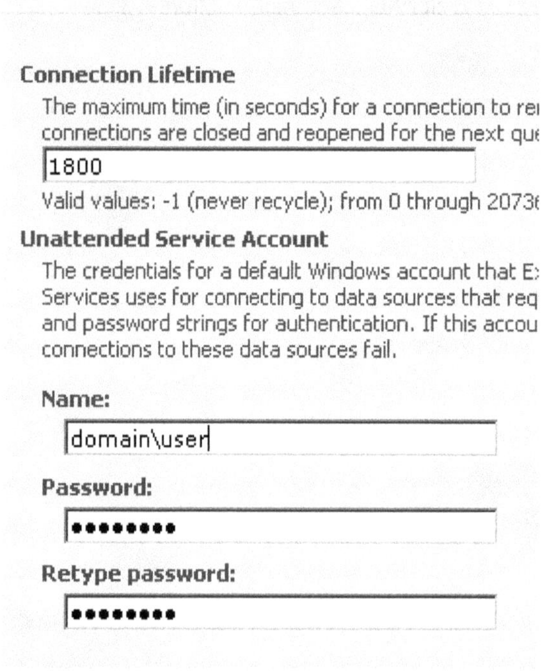

Connection Lifetime

The maximum time (in seconds) for a connection to rei
connections are closed and reopened for the next que

```
1800
```

Valid values: -1 (never recycle); from 0 through 2073€

Unattended Service Account

The credentials for a default Windows account that E:
Services uses for connecting to data sources that req
and password strings for authentication. If this accou
connections to these data sources fail.

Name:

```
domain\user
```

Password:

```
••••••••
```

Retype password:

```
••••••••
```

Figure 4.4: *Service Account settings*

Click **OK** to save changes.

4. Click **Trusted File Locations** (See figure in Step 2)

5. Click **Add Trusted File Location**.

6. Add site URL in the **Address** box and select **Windows SharePoint Services** in the "Location Type". Depending on your requirements, you can select other options, for example, if you want to access files from a UNC then "Location Type" should be **UNC**. Check **Children trusted** check box.

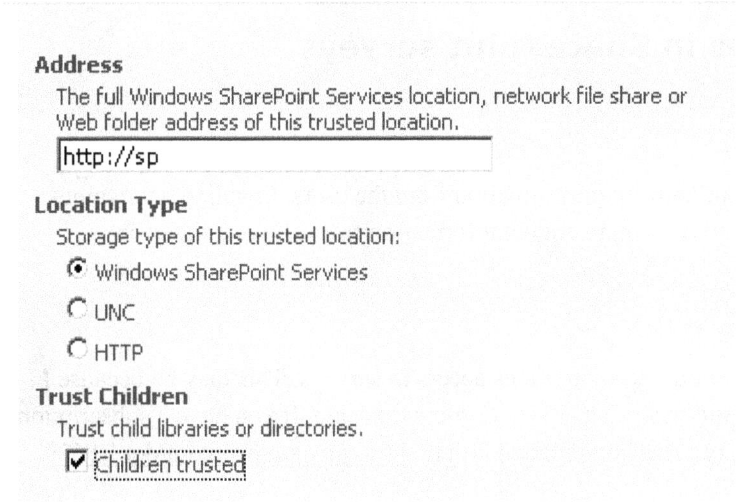

Address

The full Windows SharePoint Services location, network file share or Web folder address of this trusted location.

http://sp

Location Type

Storage type of this trusted location:

- ⦿ Windows SharePoint Services
- ○ UNC
- ○ HTTP

Trust Children

Trust child libraries or directories.

- ☑ Children trusted

Figure 4.5: *More settings*

In "External Data" section, select **Trusted data connection libraries and embedded** (Allow External Data section).

Click **OK** to save changes.

Now, you can access Excel files in SharePoint.

Anonymous access in SharePoint surveys

Introduction

Surveys are an excellent way of collecting information from the users. Enabling anonymous access in SharePoint surveys allows you to collect information from all your site visitors.

Details

I have been asked quite often about the anonymous access in surveys. This may be because I wrote a couple articles about surveys in MOSS 2007 some time ago. If you have a subscription to the Advisor magazine, you can read my detailed article (http://my.advisor.com/doc/18629) about SharePoint surveys.

Enabling anonymous access in surveys is easy. All you have to do is make some changes in the SharePoint Central Administration and the site where the survey is hosted. Following are the detailed steps required to do this:

1. Go to IIS settings. Select the SharePoint site for which you want to enable anonymous access. Select "Properties". Select "Directory Security" and enable anonymous access by checking the "Enable anonymous access" option. Use "IUSR_MACHINENAME" as the user (If your machine name is "DEV", this user name will be "IUSR_DEV".)

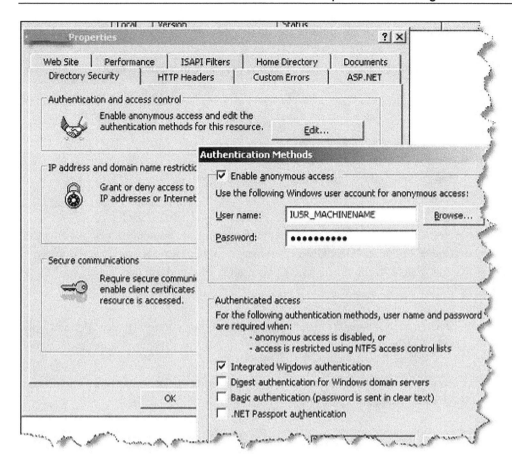

Figure 4.6: *Authentication settings*

2. Go to SharePoint Central Administration. Select "Application Management". Select "Authentication providers" under "Application Security".

3. Select correct web application from the drop down. Click "Default" zone.

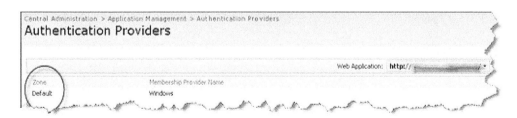

Figure 4.7: *Authentication Providers*

4. Check "Enable anonymous access" option.

5. Create a group for anonymous users at site level and assign "Contributor" rights.

Creating a group for anonymous users:

a. Open SharePoint site that hosts the survey.

b. Go to Site Actions > Site Settings and select "People and groups" from the "Users and Permissions" section.

c. Select New > New Group. Give this group a name, for example, "anon users". Scroll down and check "Contribute" option in "Give Group Permission to this Site" section. If you don't want the users to have the "delete" right, create a new permission level and use that instead of the "Contribute" option.

6. Open your survey. Go to "Settings". Click "Permissions for this survey" (under "Permissions and Management").

7. Select "Anonymous Access" from "Settings" drop down. Select permissions that you will like to give to the anonymous users and click OK.

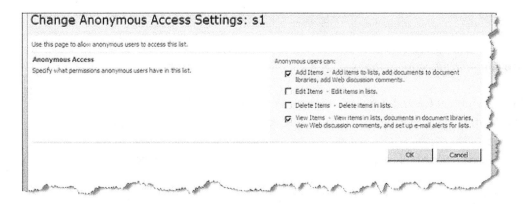

Figure 4.8: *Anonymous Access Settings*

8. Log out and access the survey list without logging in again and test the user access. You should be able to respond to a question without logging in.

Microsoft GroupBoard Workspace

"The GroupBoard Workspace template for Microsoft Windows SharePoint Services 3.0 creates a space for a group or team to connect and share information in a collaborative environment, improving team efficiency and productivity." ... Excerpt from Microsoft site:

(http://www.microsoft.com/downloads/details.aspx?familyid=4030d847-31bc-43ea-90ec-111b546d5411&displaylang=en)

Download this workspace from the following link:

http://www.microsoft.com/downloads/details.aspx?familyid=4030d847-31bc-43ea-90ec-111b546d5411&displaylang=en

Here is a screenshot:

Figure 4.9: *GroupBoard Workspace*

It's an amazing application, very easy to use! The features I liked most are:

-Schedules and Reservations
-Time Card

Create a new appointment and it will appear immediately in the "Schedule and Reservations" and "What's new" parts.

The following figure shows a web part in the "New Appointment" page. This chart helps users to select the begin and end date and time for the appointment.

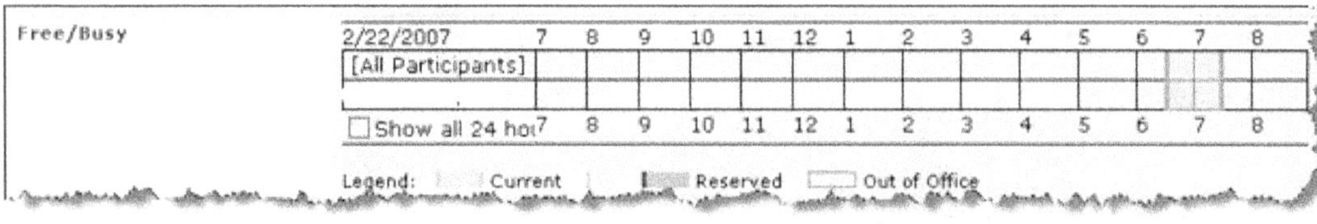

Free/Busy	2/22/2007	7	8	9	10	11	12	1	2	3	4	5	6	7	8
	[All Participants]														
	Show all 24 hou	7	8	9	10	11	12	1	2	3	4	5	6	7	8

Legend: Current   Reserved   Out of Office

Figure 4.10: *Appointments*

Entering time in time card is a one click process.

Figure 4.11: *Time Card Links*

Click **Start** to register "Time-in" and click **Return** to register "Time-out". That's it. Time card automatically calculates all other necessary information.

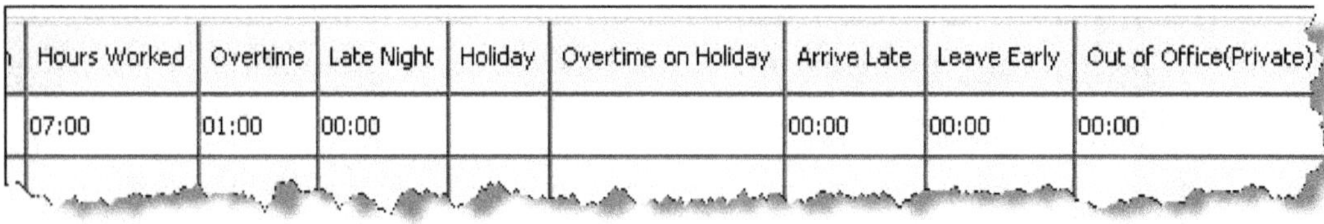

Hours Worked	Overtime	Late Night	Holiday	Overtime on Holiday	Arrive Late	Leave Early	Out of Office(Private)
07:00	01:00	00:00			00:00	00:00	00:00

Figure 4.12: *Time Card View*

You can modify time card settings in the **Settings** page.

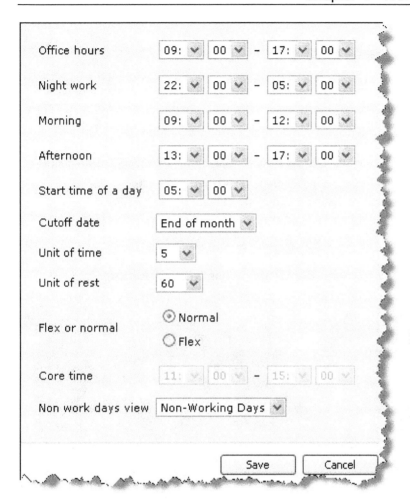

Figure 4.13: *Settings*

Sales Account Manager

Sales Account Manager is a role based template. This template can be installed on a single machine as well as multiple machines. I installed it using the second approach. My SQL Server machine is different than my SharePoint server machine. Template comes with detailed setup instructions but believe me installing and configuring it is a cumbersome task. Sales and Marketing people will love this template. I faced some problems during database installation. Setup instructions (Section 2.4 Database Installation, Page 5) tell you to copy **MySiteAccountManagerRole.bak** file in the following folder:

<Drive name>:\Program Files\Microsoft SQL Server\MSSQL.1\MSSQL\Backup

I got following error when I ran the **osql -E -i MySiteAccountManagerRole.sql**:

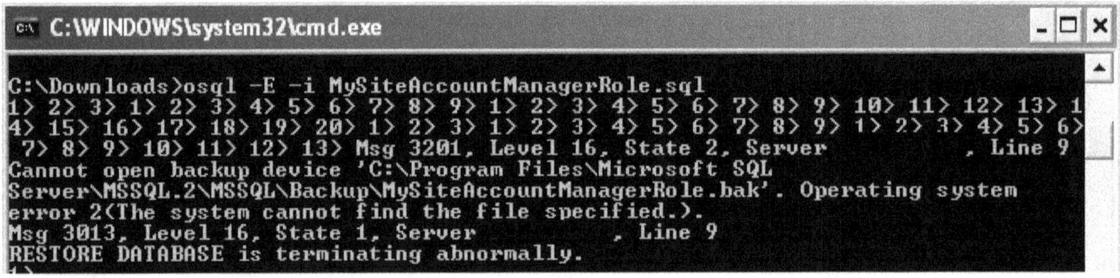

Figure 4.14: *SQL error*

Copying the **MySiteAccountManagerRole.bak** to the following folder solved my problem:

<Drive name>:\Program Files\Microsoft SQL Server\MSSQL.2\MSSQL\Backup

Another problem that I faced was that I couldn't find the .odc file mentioned in **Section 2.7.3 Document Library Settings - Step 4** and therefore, I had to update the .odc connection file manually.

Here are some screen shots of the template:

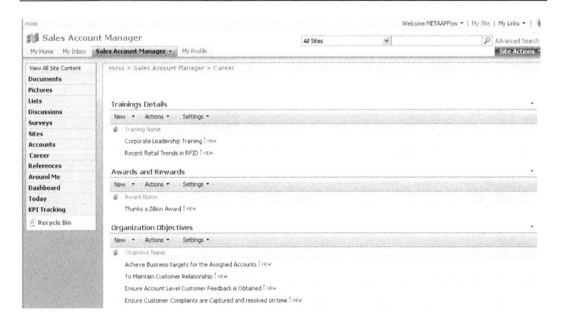

Figure 4.15: *Sales Account Manager – Screenshot 1*

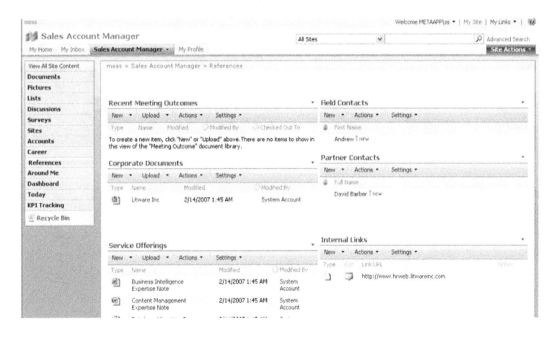

Figure 4.16: *Sales Account Manager – Screenshot 2*

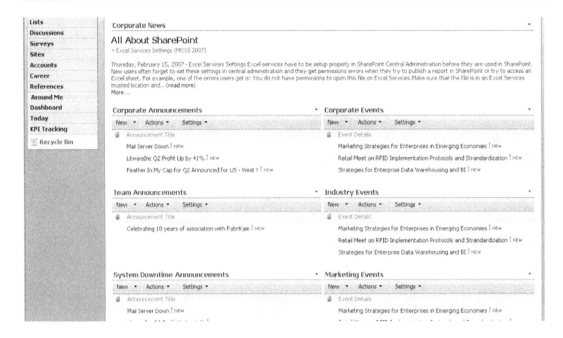

Figure 4.17: *Sales Account Manager – Screenshot 3*

Figure 4.18: *Sales Account Manager – Screenshot 4*

Displaying library items for a specific time period.

Problem: Displaying library items for a specific time period.

Scenario: Display new items in a library for 7 days. The items should disappear from the library automatically after 7 days.

Solution:

1. Open the document library where you want to make the changes.

2. Select **Create Column** from the **Settings** dropdown.

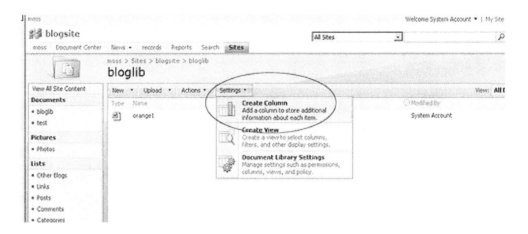

Figure 4.19: *Settings*

3. Enter "HiddenDate" in the **Column name** and select "Date and Time" as the type of information for this column. **Date and Time Format** should be "Date Only". **Default Value** should be a calculated value. Add "=Today + 7" in the **Calculated Value** field. Clear the **Add to default view** check box. Click **OK** to save the settings.

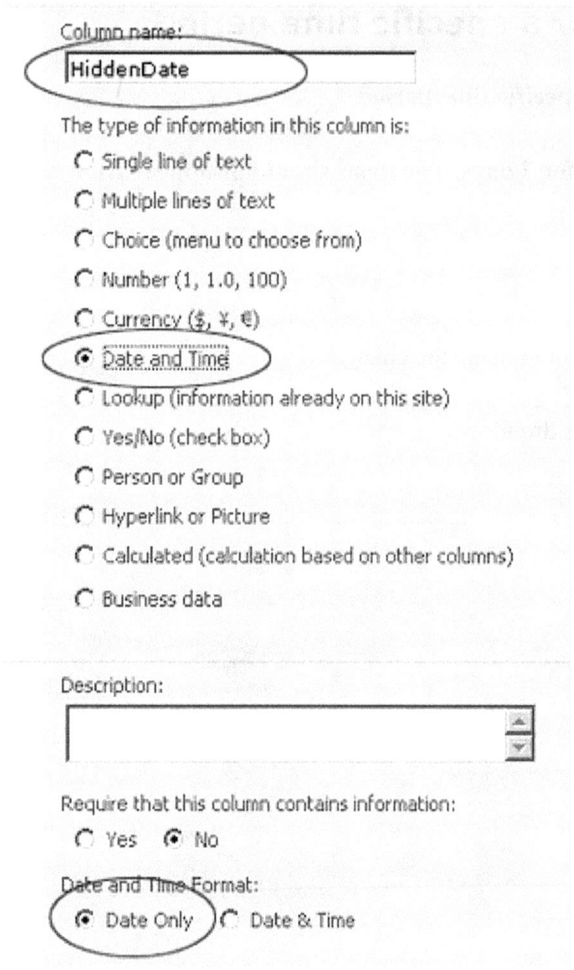

Figure 4.20: *Date column settings*

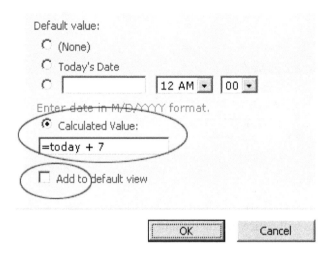

Figure 4.21: *Calculated Value*

4. Next step is to add a filter. You can add a filter to the current view or you can create a new view for this task. Select **Modify this View** from the "View" drop down.

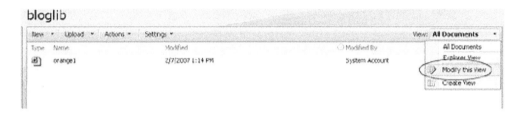

Figure 4.22: *Modify view*

5. To add a filter to the selected view, select "Show items only when the following is true". Select **HiddenDate** from the columns drop down. Select **is greater than or equal to** from the conditions' drop down and enter **[Today]** in the parameter box. Click **OK** to save the changes.

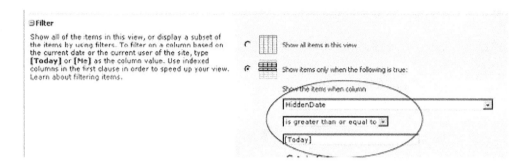

Figure 4.23: *Apply filter*

6. Now, go back to the main page and you will notice that all documents older than 7 days have disappeared.

MOSS 2007 and Code Access Security

Figure 4.24: *Code Access Security*

Download Sample Custom Policy File:

http://www.codeplex.com/wsuploadservice/Project/FileDownload.aspx?DownloadId=5518

Have you ever written a web part or a web service? If yes then you must have dealt with a security problem. Writing a web part or web service may not be a big issue but deploying them is certainly a headache. You start getting permission errors as soon as you deploy your code on the server. There are three ways to assign execution permissions to your code:

1. Increase the trust level for the entire virtual server
2. Create a custom policy file for your assemblies
3. Install your assemblies in the GAC

Safest method to install an assembly is to create a custom policy file for the assembly. Following article on MSDN contains complete details on code access security:

Microsoft Windows SharePoint Services and Code Access Security
(http://msdn2.microsoft.com/en-us/library/ms916855.aspx)

Written in July 2003, this is one of the most comprehensive articles written on "SharePoint and Code Access Security".

For security reasons, the assembly must be installed in the **bin** directory of the application instead of GAC but installing it in the **bin** directory requires you to assign execution permissions to the assembly. One way is to increase the trust level of the entire virtual server.

This is easy to implement but this option is least secure as it affects all assemblies used by that virtual server. Second way is to create a custom policy file and this is the recommended approach. This option is most secure but difficult to implement. In this section, we will create a custom policy file for an assembly (We will use WSUploadService discussed earlier in this book) written for MOSS 2007.

Creating a Custom Policy File

1. Go to the following location on the server:

LocalDrive:\Program Files\Common Files\Microsoft Shared\web server extensions\12\CONFIG

2. Make a copy of wss_minimaltrust.config and rename it wss_customtrust.config.

3. Open wss_customtrust.config file using any text editor.

4. Under the <SecurityClasses> element, add a reference to the **SharePointPermissions** class as follows:

```
<SecurityClass Name="SharePointPermission"
Description="Microsoft.SharePoint.Security.SharePointPermission,
Microsoft.SharePoint.Security, Version=12.0.0.0, Culture=neutral,
PublicKeyToken=71e9bce111e9429c." />
```

Listing 4.1: *Change in <SecurityClass>*

5. Search for the <PermissionSet> tag where the **name** attribute equals **ASP.NET**. If you couldn't find that <PermissionSet> tag, locate the one that has **SPRestricted** in the **name** attribute.

6. Copy the entire tag and all of its children, and paste a copy of it immediately below the one you copied.

7. Change the name of the **PermissionSet** element from **ASP.NET** (or **SPRestricted**) to **CustomTrust**.

Before:

```
<PermissionSet
class="NamedPermissionSet"
version="1"
Name="SPRestricted">
```

Listing 4.2: *Permissionset*

After:

```
<PermissionSet
class="NamedPermissionSet"
version="1"
Name="CustomTrust">
```

Listing 4.3: *Permissionset after modification*

8. Add the following <IPermission> node to the <PermissionSet> element where the name attribute equals **CustomTrust:**

```
<IPermission class="SharePointPermission"
version="1"
ObjectModel="True" />
```

Listing 4.4: *Add <IPermission>*

Therefore, the resulting customized <PermissionSet> will look as follows:

```
<PermissionSet
class="NamedPermissionSet"
version="1"
Name="CustomTrust">

<IPermission
class="AspNetHostingPermission"
version="1" Level="Minimal"
/>

<IPermission
class="SecurityPermission"
version="1" Flags="Execution"
/> <IPermission class="WebPartPermission"
version="1"
Connections="True"
/>

<IPermission class="SharePointPermission"
version="1"
ObjectModel="True" />
</PermissionSet>
```

Listing 4.5: *Customized permissionset*

9. Once you define the customized element, you must create a code group to specify when the CLR should apply the permission set. Locate <CodeGroup> tag where the **class** attribute equals **FirstMatchCodeGroup** and copy following **CodeGroup** immediately below it:

```
<CodeGroup class="UnionCodeGroup"
version="1"
PermissionSetName="CustomTrust">
<IMembershipCondition class="UrlMembershipCondition"
version="1"
Url="$AppDirUrl$/bin/*" />
</CodeGroup>
```

Listing 4.6: *<CodeGroup>*

The membership condition for this new code group is based on URL membership and the URL points to the **bin** directory. The permissions will be applied to all the assemblies in the **bin** directory of the current application. You can also use strong name membership but then the permissions will be applied only to one assembly. For example, if I have written a web service and I wanted to assign permissions to my assembly only, I would use strong name membership. Copy following code immediately below the <CodeGroup> tag where the **class** attribute equals **FirstMatchCodeGroup**, if you want to use strong name membership:

```
<CodeGroup class="UnionCodeGroup"
version="1"
PermissionSetName="CustomTrust">
<IMembershipCondition class="StrongNameMembershipCondition"
version="1"
PublicKeyBlob="0x00240000048000009400000006020000002400005253413100040000010001004"
Name="UploadService" />
</CodeGroup>
```

Listing 4.7: *<CodeGroup> modification*

Replace **PublicKeyBlob** value with your own value and change the name of the assembly in the **Name** attribute. **Name** attribute contains the name of the assembly. To retrieve the public key blob for an assembly, use the secutil.exe tool. Please note that **publickeyblob** is different from **publickeytoken**. Secutil.exe is located in the following folder:

LocalDrive:\Program Files\Microsoft Visual Studio 8\SDK\v2.0\Bin

To retrieve the public key blob for your assembly, either copy the secutil.exe tool to the folder that contains your assembly else provide exact path to the assembly in the command, and run the tool as follows:

```
secutil.exe -hex -s UploadService.dll > blob.txt
```

Listing 4.8: *secutil.exe*

UploadService.dll is the name of the assembly. This command will create a text file named blob.txt. Open blob.txt and copy the public key and paste it in the **publickeyblob** attribute.

10. Save and close the file. The policy file is ready to use.

11. Open the web.config file for the virtual server where you have deployed your component and add the following <trustlevel> tag to the **SecurityPolicy** element:

```
<trustLevel name="WSS_Custom" policyFile="LocalDrive:\Program Files\Common Files\Microsoft Shared\Web Server Extensions\12\config\wss_customtrust.config" />
```

Listing 4.9: *<TrustLevel>*

Virtual Directories for web applications are located in the following folder:

LocalDrive:\Inetpub\wwwroot\wss\VirtualDirectories

Suppose I want to deploy my web service in the web application configured at port 17316. The URL of that application would be http://localhost:17316/ and its virtual directory will be:

LocalDrive:\Inetpub\wwwroot\wss\VirtualDirectories\17315

Create a **bin** folder in this path and copy your assembly to the bin folder. The web.config for this virtual server will be located in the following folder:

LocalDrive:\Inetpub\wwwroot\wss\VirtualDirectories\17315

In the web.config file, change the <trust> tag so that it refers to the newly defined trust level.

```
<trust level="WSS_Custom" originUrl="" />
```

Listing 4.10: *WSS_Custom trust level*

12. Save and close the web.config file.

13. Restart IIS to apply the custom policy to the specified virtual server.

Download Sample Custom Policy File:

http://www.codeplex.com/wsuploadservice/Project/FileDownload.aspx?DownloadId=5518

Summary

This chapter was the amalgamation of different features and techniques. The chapter started with the topic that showed you how to make Excel services work in SharePoint. It talks about some important settings that are usually overlooked by the users and the services fail to work as a result. This chapter teaches you making SharePoint surveys accessible to the anonymous users. This chapter also introduced you to two very useful templates, GroupBoard Workspace and Sales Account Manager. You saw different features available out of the box in these two extremely useful templates. This chapter also teaches you a technique to hide library items after a certain amount of time. The last section is about the code access security. This is another area that is overlooked by the users but is of great importance, especially to the developers who struggle to apply code access security to their components. Developing components for SharePoint is only half work, the remaining work is to use them with proper security settings in a proper security context.

Chapter 5

Working with SharePoint Search

In this chapter:

- Customize SharePoint Search Interface
- Customize search results page
- Searching Fileshares in MOSS 2007

Customize SharePoint Search Interface

In this walk through, you will learn how to customize the default SharePoint search interface by adding new tabs:

a. You will add a new content source.

b. You will add a new scope and add rules for this new scope.

c. You will add a new tab in the search center on your SharePoint site and create search pages for this tab.

d. Finally, you will publish your changes to SharePoint.

1. Open SharePoint Central Administration and select a Shared Services Provider. If you haven't created a SSP yet, follow the instructions given in chapter 2.

2. Click **Search Settings**.

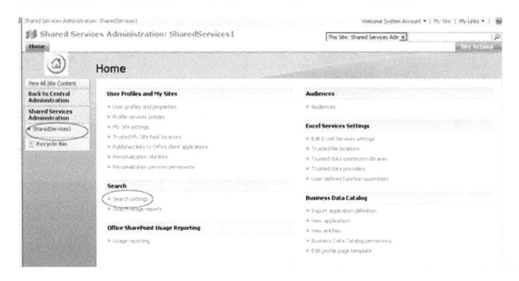

Figure 5.1: *Shared Services*

3. Click **Content sources and crawl schedules** in search settings.

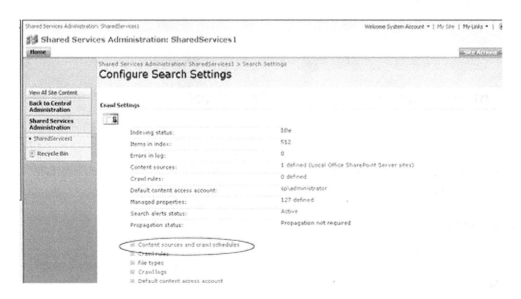

Figure 5.2: *Configure Search Settings*

4. If there is no content source available, add a new one by clicking **New Content Source**. By default, **Local Office SharePoint Server sites** is available. Open the content source's context menu by left-clicking the down arrow and select **Start Full Crawl** to index all files. This will start the indexing process.

Figure 5.3: *Manage Content Sources*

5. Click **View Crawl Log** from the same context menu to view the processing.

Figure 5.4: *Crawl Log*

Had there been any error, a red icon (circle) would have been shown here. This page will show the status of the indexing process.

6. Go back to the search settings page and click **View scopes** link in the Scopes section. On the page that opens, click **New Scope**. In the **Title**, add "My Documents". In the **Description** field, add some description and click **OK**.

Figure 5.5: *Scopes*

7. Following page will appear:

Figure 5.6: *Add Rules*

Note that **Update Status** shows "Empty" against the newly added scope (**My Documents**). Click **Add rules** link to specify rules for this scope. Select **Web Address** radio button and enter a web address in the **folder** text box. This will be the web address of the site you want to search. Click **OK**.

Figure 5.7: *Add Scope Rule*

8. You will notice that the new scope has been added but indexing is still pending.

Figure 5.8: *Indexing is pending*

To start indexing immediately, go to **Search Settings** page and click **Start update now** link (**Scopes** section).

9. Go to the search center of your SharePoint site and add a new tab to search the newly added scope but wait .. before adding a new tab we need to create two pages, one for search and the other for search results.

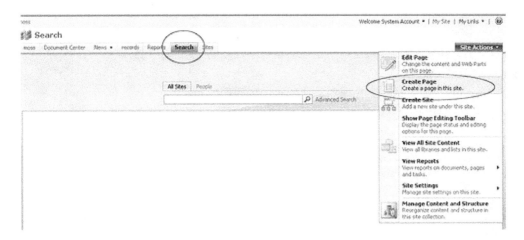

Figure 5.9: *Search Tab*

Go to **Site Actions** and select **Create Page**.

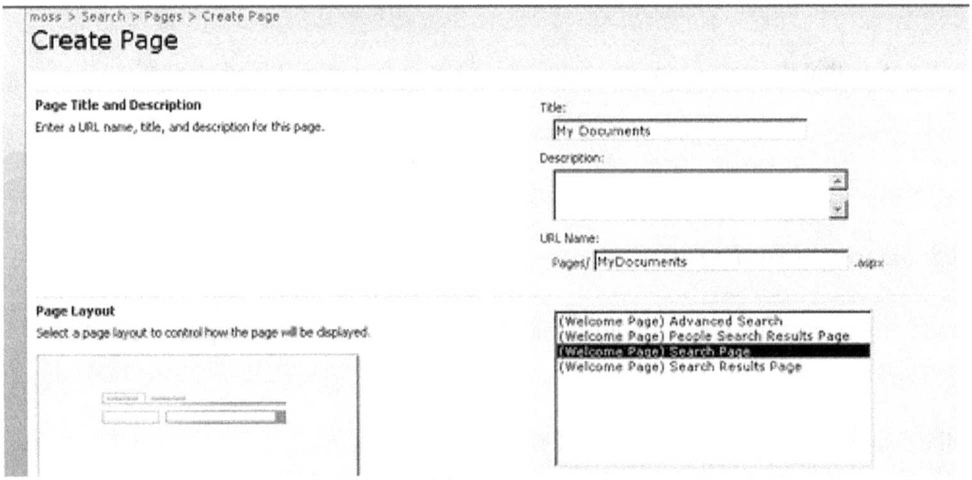

Figure 5.10: *Create Search Page*

Enter "My Documents" in the **Title** field and enter "MyDocuments" in the **URL Name** field. In fact, SharePoint will automatically add the URL name but of course, you can change the page name to your liking. Select "(Welcome Page) Search Page" from the **Page Layout** box and click the **Create** button.

10. Click **Add New Tab** link.

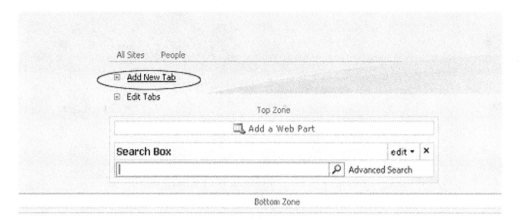

Figure 5.11: *Add New Tab*

Enter "My Documents" in the **Tab Name** field and "mydocuments.aspx" in the **Page** field and "Search your favorite documents" in the **Tooltip** field and click **OK**.

11. Now, the second step is to create the search results page for the tab we just added. Again, select **Create Page** from the **Site Actions**. Enter "My Documents Results" in the **Title** field. Enter "mydocumentsresults" in the **URL Name** field. Select "Search Results Page" from the **Page Layout** box and click the **Create** button.

12. On the page that opens, click the **Add New Tab** link. Enter "My Documents" in the **Tab Name** field and "mydocumentsresults.aspx" in the **Page** field and click **OK**.

13. Click the **edit** link in the search box and select **Modify Shared Web Part**. This will open the properties page for the search box. Expand **Miscellaneous** and enter "mydocumentsresults.aspx" in the **Target search results page URL**. By default, this field contains **results.aspx**.

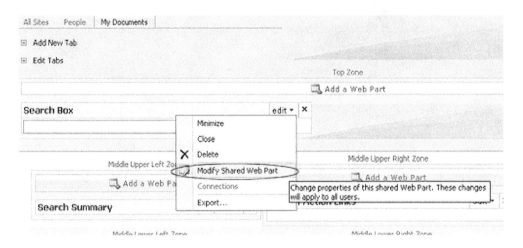

Figure 5.12: *My Documents*

14. On the same page, there is another web part called as **Search Core Results**. Click the **edit** button in this web part and select **Modify Shared Web Part**. Expand **Miscellaneous** and enter the name of the scope that you created in the previous steps (**My Documents**). Once you have done that, it's time to publish the page. Click **Check In to Share Draft** link.

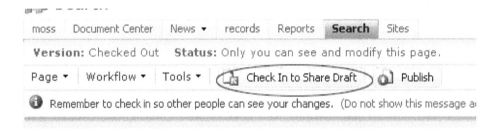

Figure 5.13: *Check In to Share Draft*

15. Try your newly added tab. Enter a keyword and click the search icon. Now, you will see results that are of interest to you. You won't see all the links in the results. Your search results have been filtered.

Customize search results page

We will customize the search results page that we created in the previous section.

1. Open the search center (Select **Search** from the tabs bar) in your SharePoint site.

2. Select **Edit Page** from the **Site Actions** menu.

3. Click the **edit** link in the **Search Box** and select **Modify Shared Web Part**. Expand **Scopes Dropdown**. There are several options listed in the **Dropdown mode** dropdown. If you want to show scopes drop down on the search page, select "Show scopes dropdown" and if you want to hide it, select "Do not show scopes dropdown". It doesn't make sense to show the scopes drop down because we are searching only one scope that we added in the previous section.

4. To increase the width of the search box, expand **Query Text Box** and add "350" in the **Query text box width** field. Click **Ok** to save the changes.

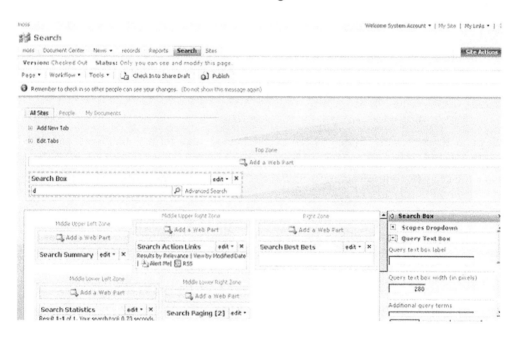

Figure 5.14: *Search Box Settings*

5. Click **edit** link in the **Search Core Results** web part and select **Modify Shared Web Part**. Expand **Results Display/Views**. Enter "5" in the **Results Per Page** field. Enter "1" in **Sentences in Summary** field. This will reduce the cluttering on the results page. Select "Modified Date" in the **Default Results View** drop down to show the results sorted by the modified date.

6. You can also modify the appearance of the results page by modifying the XSL. Click the **XSL Editor...** button to open the editor. You will notice there are different sections in the stylesheet. You can change image paths in this stylesheet. You can also modify the text messages that appear on the results page.

7. Click **Check In to Share Draft** link to publish the changes. You will see the changes that you just made on the results page. There will be only 5 rows, only 1 line summary, etc.

There are some more interesting features related to search that we can take advantage of. For example, SharePoint provides a way to view search usage reports. We all know how important reports are for the administrators, senior managers and executives. Let's explore some of these great features.

1. Open **SharePoint Central Administration** and click on the Shared Services link. Depending on your needs, you can create more than one SSP. Click on **Search usage reports** to view some interesting reports. This page shows following reports:

a. Queries over previous 30 days
b. Queries over past 12 months
c. Top query origin site collections over previous 30 days
d. Queries per scope over previous 30 days
e. Top queries over previous 30 days

Good thing about these reports is that you can export them to other formats like Excel and PDF. For example, select "Acrobat(PDF) File" from the **Select a format** dropdown and click the **Export** link located next to the dropdown. SharePoint will prompt you to open or save the document.

2. Another nice feature in SharePoint Search is the **Search Result Removal**. Suppose some one mistakenly uploaded a confidential document which should not have been published and you, as an administrator, want to remove the document from the search results. What will you do? Click **Search settings** on the Shared services page. Under **Crawl Settings**, select **Search result removal**. Enter the path of the confidential document in the **URLs to remove** and click **Remove Now** button. That's it! The link(s) will be immediately removed from the index and yes, there is no need to start the crawl to re-index the site.

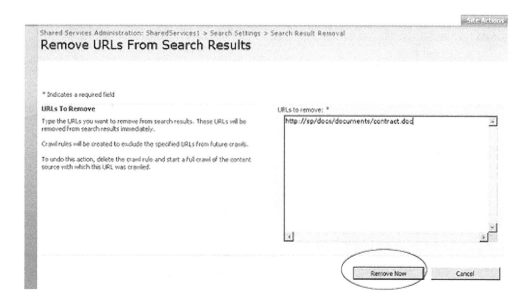

Figure 5.15: *Remove URLs From Search Results*

3. There are some more useful reports that I forgot to mention. On **shared services** page, click **Search usage reports**. Click **Search results** from the **Search usage reports** box on the left. This view shows following reports:

a. Search Results Top Destination Pages
b. Queries With Zero Results
c. Most Clicked Best Bets
d. Queries With Zero Best Bets
e. Queries With Low Clickthrough

4. You can create crawl rules of your own. On the **Configure Search Settings** page, click **Crawl rules** link and then click **New Crawl Rule**.

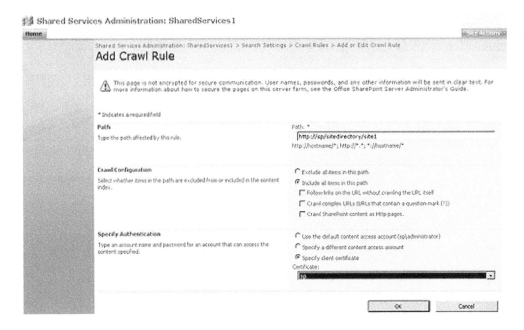

Figure 5.16: *Add Crawl Rule*

Enter a path in the **Path** field. You can exclude or include this path from the crawl process depending on your requirements. If you select **Exclude all items in this path**, all other options on this page will be grayed out. In that case, this path will not be included in the crawl process. If you include it in the indexing process, then you can make some more configurations which can be seen in the above figure. For example, you can enable the **Crawl complex URLs** option to include all types of URLs in the indexing process. You can also specify authentication and not only that, you can also select a certificate from the drop down if you select the **Specify client certificate** option.

5. You can enable or disable search based alerts by clicking the **Search-based alerts** link on the **Configure Search Settings** page.

Well, these were some of the nice features that are part of the latest SharePoint portal server. I am sure administrators will love these features.

Searching Fileshares in MOSS 2007

Searching fileshares in MOSS 2007 is very easy. I always considered this feature to be very useful and this was one of my favorite features in SPS 2003. Following are the steps (with screenshots) required to create a fileshare in MOSS 2007:

1. Go to "SharePoint Central Administration" and select a "Shared Service" that is associated with the application in which you want to show the results of a fileshare search. You can create a new "Shared Service" as well if you intend to create a new application. You can also associate your existing "Shared Service" with the new (to be created) sites. To do this, go to "Shared Services Administration" and change the default SSP by clicking "Change Default SSP". This will automatically associate your newly created sites with an existing (default) SSP.

Figure 5.17: *Central Administration*

2. In your selected SSP, click the "Search Settings" link.

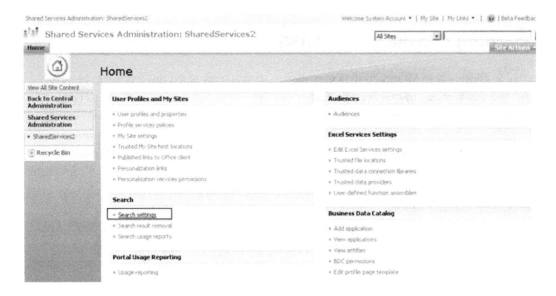

Figure 5.18: *Search settings*

3. In the "Configure Search Settings" page, click the "Content sources" link.

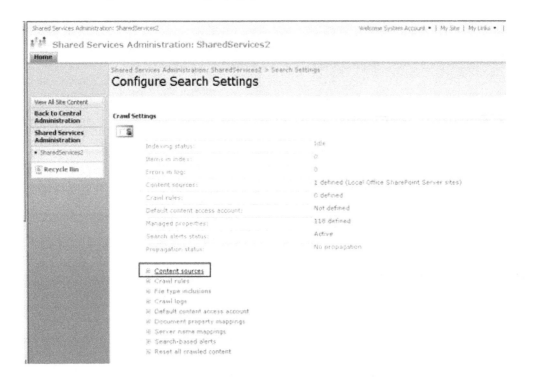

Figure 5.19: *Content sources*

4. In the "Manage Content Sources" page, click the "New Content Source" link.

Figure 5.20: *Manage Content Sources*

5. Add a name for your content source in the "Name:" field and select "File Shares" as the content type. In the start address box, add your fileshare. This should be a shared folder, for example, \\sp\test. In this case, "sp" is your machine name and "test" is the shared folder on machine "sp".

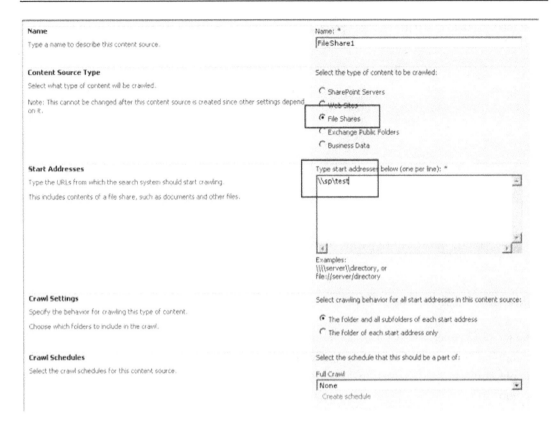

Figure 5.21: *Search Settings*

6. Check the "Start full crawl of this content source" checkbox and click "OK". "Manage Content Sources" page will show the status as "Crawling Full". Refresh the page and you will notice that the status has been changed to "Idle". Crawling might take some time, depending on the size of the shared folder.

7. Now, go to your SharePoint site and try to find a file using a keyword in the search box. SharePoint will return the file against the keyword you enter.

Summary

This chapter discussed search interface in SharePoint in detail. You learned how to customize the search interface. You also learned how to customize the search results page. An important topic of searching file shares was also discussed in this chapter. Some people tend to use SharePoint only so that they can search their documents. For this they import all documents into SharePoint. That is not required if your only objective is to search the documents. You can still search the documents while keeping them on your hard disk. This chapter showed you how.

116

Chapter 6

SharePoint and InfoPath

In this chapter:

- Inspecting logic and checking design of InfoPath forms
- Deploying InfoPath forms
- Populating multi-select list box in InfoPath 2007 web forms programmatically
- Working with InfoPath radio buttons and check boxes
- Copying file attachments from one section to another in InfoPath
- Managing older versions of InfoPath forms
- Creating a filtered column in InfoPath (data from a SharePoint list)
- Submitting InfoPath data to a SharePoint list
- Creating web enabled InfoPath forms
- Publishing InfoPath web form using stsadm command line utility
- Programming InfoPath web forms
- Populating InfoPath drop down with SharePoint list data
- Retrieving data from a SharePoint list
- Retrieving data from a SharePoint list using SPQuery
- Showing filtered items in InfoPath drop down

Inspecting Logic and Checking Design of InfoPath Form

It is easier to inspect the logic manually in simple forms but companies use InfoPath not to create simple forms but to create forms in an easy and simple way. These forms can get quite complex and large. Once developed and deployed, there are different techniques that developers can use to track down errors but even at design time inspecting and fixing errors in the form can be a tedious job. Forms can have hundreds of nodes or may be 20-30 fields in a single view. It's not easy to find problems with the data sources without the help of a tool. Unfortunately, logic inspector and design checker, tools that come with InfoPath are usually overlooked and not taken advantage of by the developers.

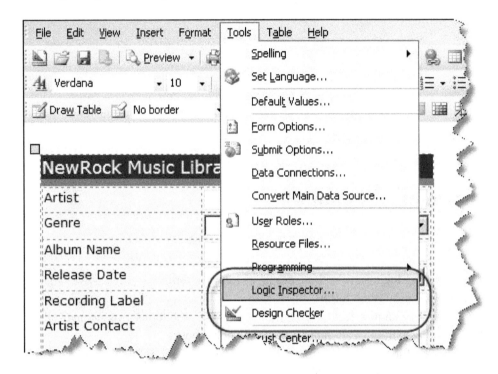

Figure 6.1: *Logic Selector can be selected from the Tools menu*

There are some errors that become evident only after when a developer tries to deploy the form. Large number of data sources or fields is not the only problem, no form is complete without the data validation checks, rules and business logic. Logic Inspector enables developers to find problems with the form before they try and deploy it on the destination server. It allows them to view the data validation checks, rules, calculated default values, and business logic, all in one place. Design Checker is another tool that can be used to check the form design for performance related issues before deploying the form. I admit, even I used to underestimate the power of this tool but It really helped me once to resolve performance issues in a large form that comprised of hundreds of nodes, validation checks, rules and thousands of lines of business logic code. Let's take a look at the Logic Inspector first before moving on towards the Design Checker.

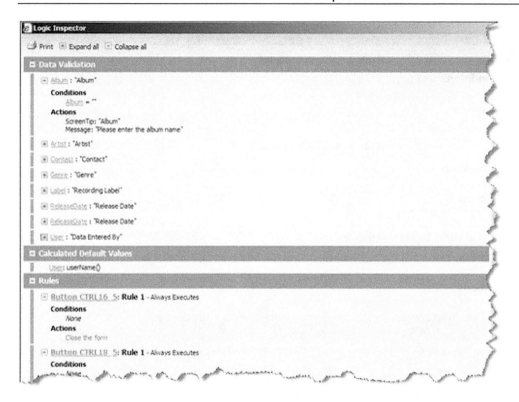

Figure 6.2: *Logic Inspector inspects Data validation, Calculated Default Values, Rules and Programming*

Logic Inspector and Design Checker can be selected from the Tools menu. Design Checker is also available in the Design Tasks pane. When you work on a large form, it is very common to delete fields and/or nodes from the form and at the same time adding new nodes or fields in the form. This can easily inject problems in your form because many of the fields are interdependent on each other. One field may be dependent on a value in another field. Now suppose you remove the field that had data that was being used in another field. You will not get any error message but when you will try to deploy the form, it will fail. Now imagine you have to find the problem manually in the form that houses hundreds of nodes and 30-40 fields in each view and there may be more than one view in your form. It will be a tedious task. Logic Inspector comes to your rescue at this point.

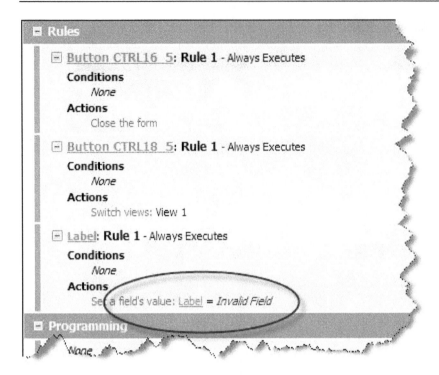

Figure 6.3: *Logic Inspector catches broken rules*

See Figure 6.3 above. "Invalid Field" message shown in red tells you that a field that was being used in a rule has been deleted. You will have to re-add the field, remove the rule or edit the rule in order to fix the problem. Your form will not publish unless you fix this problem.

You can run Logic Inspector to view the logic in the complete form or you can also invoke it to inspect logic in a single field.

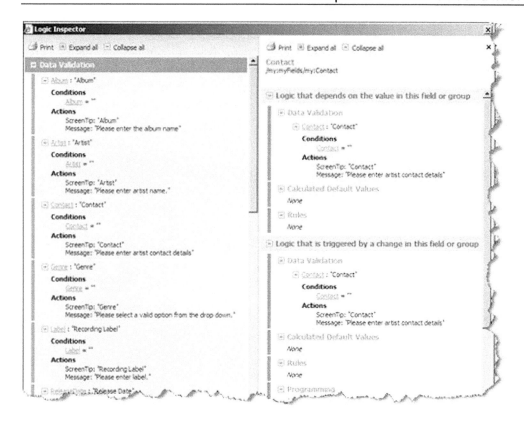

Figure 6.4: *Logic Inspector can be invoked for a single field*

To inspect a single field, right click the field and select "Logic Inspector". It will show you the complete details, for example, there will be a section called "Logic that depends on the value in this field group". There will be another one called "Logic that is triggered by a change in this field or group". (See Figure 6.4). You can also view logic for a single field by clicking the "Field Name" hyperlink. It will open another pane to the right that will show you the details.

Now let's turn towards the Design Checker. Design Checker is another very important tool that you should not miss when working on a complex form. Performance may not matter in case of small forms but it really matters when one is developing a complex form. Creating nested sections, nested tables, nested nodes is a very common scenario in complex forms. This is where developers usually make a mistake without thinking about the implications that will affect the form's performance. Especially if it's a web enabled form that will run in a browser, then of course you can not comprise on the form's performance. No one will know the difference when opening the form in the InfoPath client application but loading the same form in a web browser will show you why it is important to take care of the performance issues. Complex forms load very slow in browsers. It can take a complex form 2 to 20 seconds or may be even more to load in a browser. Well, that's a lot of time and you won't believe how annoying it becomes when the form takes so much time to load. You can reduce this loading time by fine tuning your form and resolving the performance issues. One mistake that developers usually make is that they don't take care of the hierarchy in which they insert the nodes in the data source. This can have serious implications. For example, if you have added **fields** to a **section** then in the nodes' hierarchy, **fields'** nodes should come under the **section's** node. Look at the figure below to get a better understanding of what I mean.

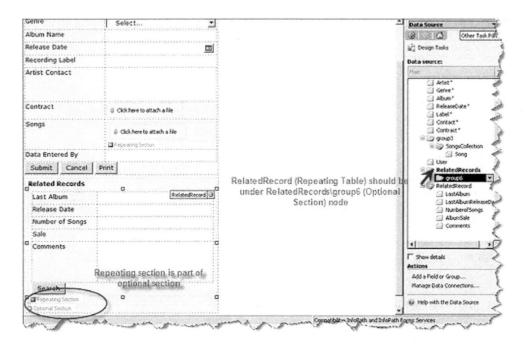

Figure 6.5: *Locate node hierarchy inconsistencies with Design Checker*

"RelatedRecord" is a repeating table and is a part of "RelatedRecords" which is a repeating section and we can see this in the design view of the form but in the data source, if you notice, the "RelatedRecord" comes under "myFields" and not under the "RelatedRecords" node. This will work. Preview the form and everything will work as expected. This is a very simple example. In real life scenarios, some times we have to use nested tables that can go up to 5 levels deep and in such cases if a developer does not take care of the hierarchy in which the fields are added to the data source then this can have serious implications as far as form's performance is concerned. Form will load very slow. If you want to read more about the performance related issues and tips on how to fine tune InfoPath forms, then there are a couple of very good articles available on Microsoft site:

Improving the Performance of InfoPath 2007 Forms (http://msdn2.microsoft.com/en-us/library/bb380251.aspx)

122

InfoPath Forms Services best practices (http://technet2.microsoft.com/Office/en-us/library/0e9966df-e374-4df5-b3be-9848c78f9ca71033.mspx?mfr=true)

If your form has hundreds of data nodes then use Design Checker to check hierarchy related inconsistencies.

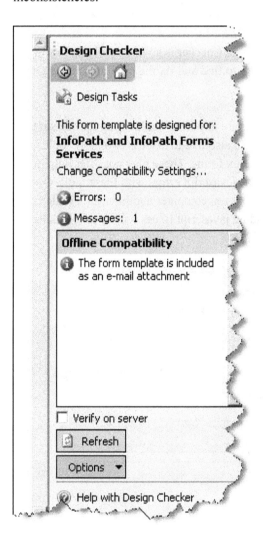

Figure 6.6: *Design Checker Pane*

All inconsistencies are shown in the "Offline Compatibility" section. To view a detailed message, click the message in this section. It will pop-up a message box that will show you the detailed message. Developers should always run Design Checker before publishing the form and should fix all issues reported by the Design Checker. Design Checker also helps in pin pointing "Online Compatibility" issues. Check the "Verify on server" option and click

"Refresh". If the publishing location is SharePoint then the Design Checker will verify if the destination site or library still exists or not. This can also help if there is an issue with any of your promoted fields. If you change the data type of a field in your form that was previously promoted to be used in a SharePoint forms library, and you forget to remove the previously promoted field and re-add it, your form will not publish and will give you an error. Again, as I said, if your form contains many fields then locating such issues becomes easier with Design Checker. Design Checker will show you the source of the error which you can then easily fix before trying to publish the form again. All in all, Design Checker is a handy tool and lots of headaches can be avoided if developers use these tools to find and fix the problems at design time.

We just saw why Logic Inspector and Design Checker are important tools for any professional developer working on complex InfoPath forms. I would also like to discuss two more tools very briefly that can be helpful in finding issues with complex forms. These may not offer help in finding the business logic issues but you can locate the javascript errors with these tools. One is Fiddler. Fiddler can be used to log all HTTP traffic between computer and Internet. Fiddler, when used with a browser, can be very useful in finding javascript issues with forms. Fiddler uses its own built-in inspector to analyze HTTP traffic.

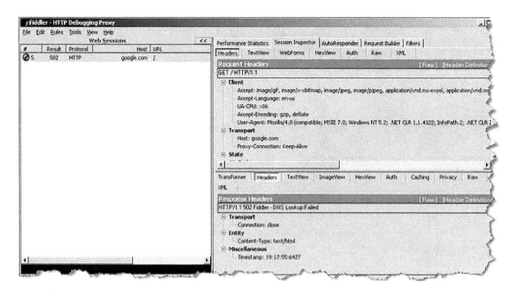

Figure 6.7: *Catch HTTP and javascript errors with Fiddler*

Another important tool is Internet Explorer Developer Toolbar (http://www.microsoft.com/downloads/details.aspx?familyid=e59c3964-672d-4511-bb3e-2d5e1db91038&displaylang=en) . IE Developer Toolbar is a must have for every web developer. It is not meant for finding issues with InfoPath forms but because web enabled

InfoPath forms load and run in a browser, developers can use it to find any javascript related errors. It allows users to explore Document Object Model (DOM) of a web page.

And finally, if you developed a form using Visual Studio then you don't need any other debugger. Built-in Visual Studio debugger is enough to find business logic and javascript related errors in your web form. Javascript error will show you the filename that contains the source of the error. You can open that file in Visual Studio and put a break point in the function that you think contains the source of the error. Visual Studio will show the exact source and the error message that you can then fix easily.

Deploying InfoPath Forms

Deploying InfoPath 2007 forms, unlike 2003 forms, is easy. My overall experience of working with InfoPath 2007 was really good. InfoPath 2007 has really matured. There are quite a few changes and deploying the forms has become very easy. Another major problem with InfoPath 2003 was that changing the development machine was very difficult. You lost many changes made to the form during the process but interestingly, InfoPath 2007 provides you a way to transfer forms from one development machine to another. Backward compatibility is also supported for InfoPath 2003 forms. You must have InfoPath 2003 Service Pack 1 to view backward compatible forms created with InfoPath 2007.

Let's create a backward compatible form in InfoPath 2007 and deploy it on a server having WSS 2.0 and InfoPath 2003:

For demo purposes, we will create a simple user registration form.

1. Open InfoPath 2007 and select **Design a Form Template** from the "File" menu.

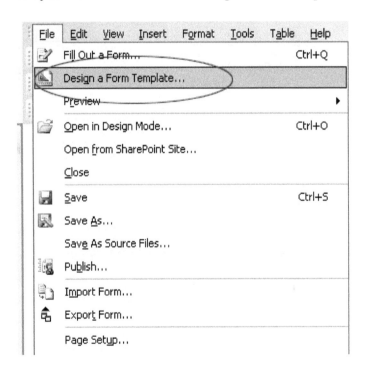

Figure 6.8: *Design a Form Template*

2. Select **Blank** template and click **OK**.

126

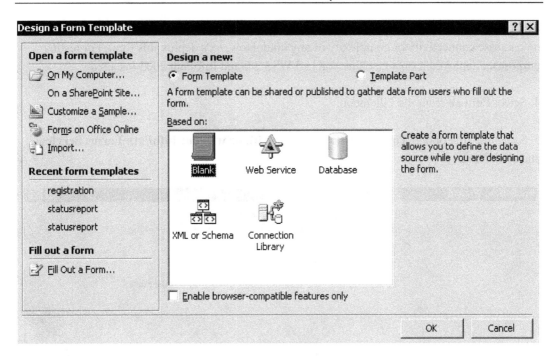

Figure 6.9: *Design Form Template*

3. Add a table with 9 rows and 2 columns and add a text box in the second column of each row. For field names, see the figure below:

Registration Form (Backward Compatible)

First Name	
Last Name	
Email	
Web	
Address	
Phone	
State	
Zip	
Country	

Submit   Cancel

Figure 6.10: *Registration Form*

Add two buttons and change the label of the buttons (See figure above). It's a simple form with no database connectivity or complexity of any kind. Now, let's deploy this form. For testing purposes, I deployed it on a machine that had WSS 2.0 and InfoPath 2003 installed.

4. Select **Publish** from the File menu.

5. Select the first option **To a SharePoint server with or without InfoPath Forms Services** and click **Next**.

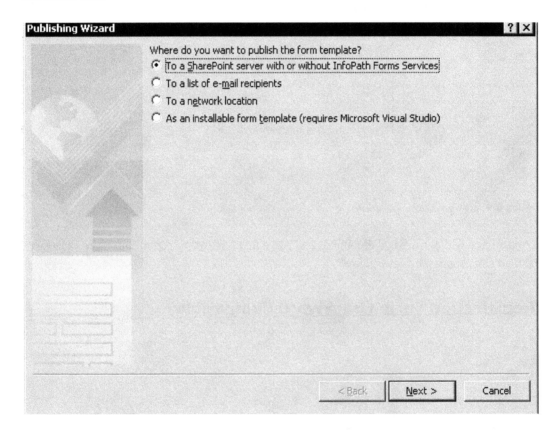

Figure 6.11: *Publishing Wizard*

6. Enter server URL in the location box and click **Next**.

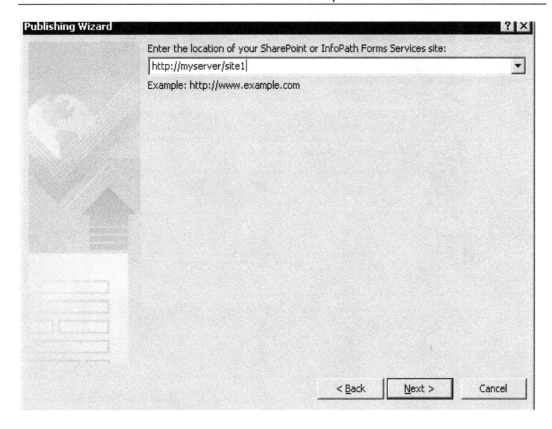

Figure 6.12: *Publishing Wizard – SharePoint Site*

7. Only one option "Document Library" will be shown because content types are not supported in older versions. Click the **Next** button to continue.

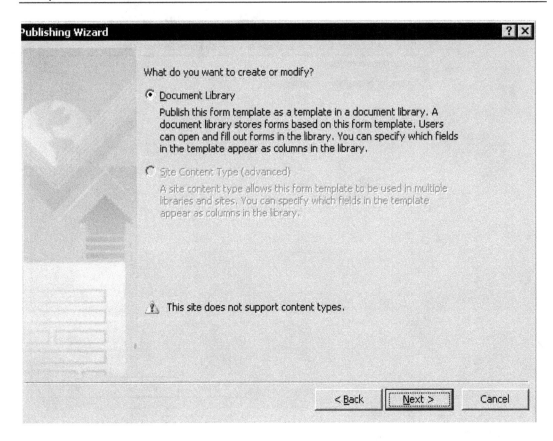

Figure 6.13: *Publishing Wizard – Document Library*

8. Select a library from the list of available libraries or create a new one. Click **Next** to continue.

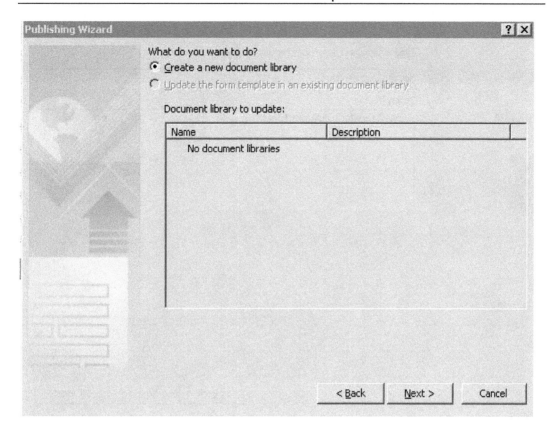

Figure 6.14: *Publishing Wizard – Create new library*

9. If you are creating a new library, enter name and description for the library and click **Next**.

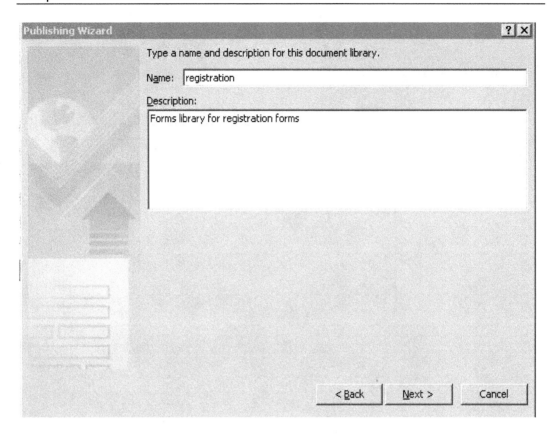

Figure 6.15: *Publishing Wizard – Name of library*

10. Click the **Add...** button to add fields from the form that you want to show in the SharePoint library. Click **Next**.

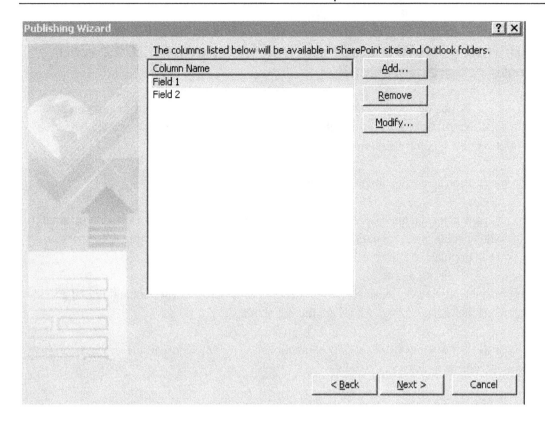

Figure 6.16: *Publishing Wizard – Add columns*

11. Click the Publish button. Depending on the security settings, you might be asked to enter your login credentials. You will see a success message. Click **Close** to close the form.

12. Open the newly created forms library on the SharePoint server to test the form.

13. Click **Fill Out This Form**.

14. This will open the form. Enter some information and save the form to the library.

Populating multi-select list box in InfoPath 2007 web forms programmatically

Multi-select list box that comes with InfoPath 2007 does not work in web forms so you have to create your own control for usage in web forms. The following article shows you how to create a multi-select list box for web forms:

http://blogs.msdn.com/infopath/archive/2004/04/01/106039.aspx

Once you have created a multi-select list box, you can add static values but what if you want to populate this list box programmatically. How will you do that? The following tip shows you how you can populate this list box programmatically:

Please read the article mentioned above before continuing because without reading that article first it won't make sense to you what I am talking about.

I will use the same names (for controls) as mentioned in the Microsoft article so that it's easier for you to understand what's happening.

For your convenience, I will list the control names here:

options: is the group name

option: is the repeating group

selected: is used for the checkbox and contains true/false value

text: is a text box and is used to store the text value

Create a navigator first to navigate the xml nodes.

```
XPathNavigator DOM = this.MainDataSource.CreateNavigator();
```

Listing 6.1: *Define navigator*

"arrayItems" is an array of items retrieved from the database. Write a function that returns an array containing the items that you want to show in the multi-select list box. I have not included that function here. It's a straight forward thing and not related directly to what I am trying to explain.

We will get the items from the array and add them to the list box. We will not touch the checkbox right now. We will just add the text values to the text boxes. By default, there is one row in the multi select list box. You must create new rows dynamically. Check the array length. If the length is 10 items, create 10 new rows. Best way is to iterate through the array and create new rows and populate the rows with the items retrieved from the array.

```
if (arrayItems.Length > 0)
{
    XPathNavigator Item =
DOM.SelectSingleNode("/my:myFields/my:options/my:option", this.NamespaceManager);

    XPathNavigator newItemNode = null;

    for (int itemIndex = 0; itemIndex < arrayItems.Length-1; itemIndex++)
    {
        if (Item != null)
        newItemNode = Item.Clone();

        XPathNavigator navText =
newItemNode.SelectSingleNode("/my:myFields/my:options/my:option/my:text",
this.NamespaceManager);

        navText.SetValue(arrayItems[itemIndex].ToString());

        Item.InsertAfter(newItemNode);

        navText = null;
        newItemNode = null;
    }

    Item.DeleteSelf();
    Item = null;
}
DOM = null;
```

Listing 6.2: *Inserting new nodes*

135

Ok, so here is what I do. I create a clone of the original row and add a value to the text box of this new row.

```
newItemNode = Item.Clone(); // create a clone
```

Listing 6.3: *Create a cloned node*

Select the text box of the newly created (cloned) row:

```
XPathNavigator navText =
newItemNode.SelectSingleNode("/my:myFields/my:options/my:option/my:text",
this.NamespaceManager);
```

Listing 6.4: *Select main node*

Set its value with the item retrieved from the array:

```
navText.SetValue(arrayItems[itemIndex].ToString());
```

Listing 6.5: *Set node value with an array item*

Likewise, if you want to check the checkboxes programmatically, set the value of the control to boolean True or False. True will check the box, and False will uncheck the box. For example, you can check the box like this:

```
XPathNavigator navCheck =
newItemNode.SelectSingleNode("/my:myFields/my:options/my:option/my:
selected", this.NamespaceManager);

navCheck.SetValue("true");
```

Listing 6.6: *Set checkbox value*

136

Working with InfoPath radio buttons and check boxes

Indeed, working with InfoPath is easy but sometimes some tips come in handy, specially when you are short on time.

We will see how you can control different sections in a form using radio buttons. Consider this scenario. You have sections in a form. Each section opens up by clicking a check box. There are radio options in the form, option 1 and option 2. When user selects option 1, checkbox 1 should be checked and section 1 should open. When user selects option 2, checkbox 2 should be checked and section 2 should open. Similarly, when user selects option 2, checkbox 1 should be unchecked and section 1 should hide. When user selects option 1, checkbox 2 should be unchecked and section 2 should hide. Fair enough! It seems easy but there is a small catch. To check a checkbox, you set its value to "True" or "1". To uncheck it, you set its value to "False" or "0". Does this work? No. To uncheck a checkbox, you should set its value to "" (blank). Setting it to "False" will not give error but desired result will not be produced. The checkbox will not be unchecked and hence related section will not hide. Also, to set a value to "True", simply writing "True" in the value will not work. You should use boolean() function. For example, boolean("True") or boolean("False"). Another interesting thing is, simply typing this formula in the value box will not work. InfoPath will treat it as a text. InfoPath will put single quotes around it and consider it text. Proper way is to use designer.

1. This is how form with controls will look like:

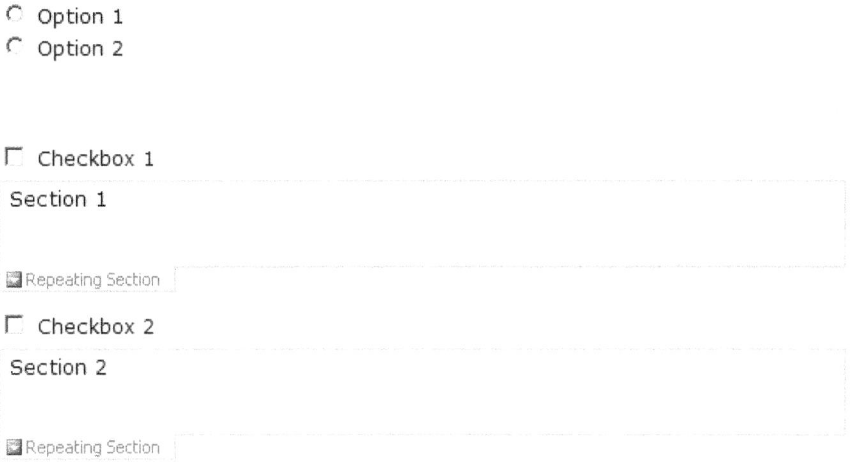

   ○ Option 1
   ○ Option 2

   ☐ Checkbox 1
   Section 1

   Repeating Section
   ☐ Checkbox 2
   Section 2

   Repeating Section

Figure 6.17: *Form*

2. Add conditional formatting to Section 1 to hide it when Checkbox 1 is checked.

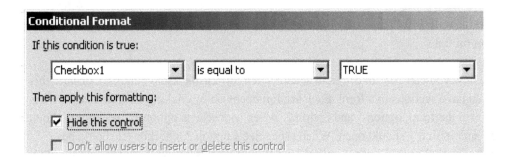

Figure 6.18: *Conditional formatting for Section 1*

3. Add conditional formatting to Section 2 to hide it when Checkbox 2 is checked.

4. Add rule to Option 1. By default, the value of Option button 1 is "1" and value of option button 2 is "2". Name rule "Open Section1" and set condition:

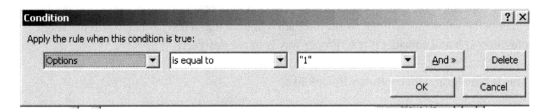

Figure 6.19: *Set condition for Rule "Open Section1"*

5. After setting the condition, click "Add Action" button to add action. In the "Field", select "Checkbox1" then click the "fx" button to add formula.

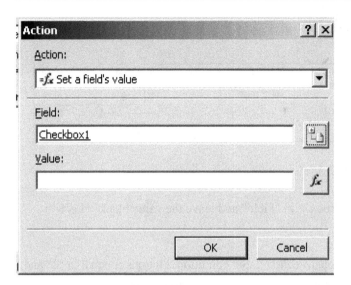

Figure 6.20: *Add Action*

6. Use "Insert Function" button to add "boolean" function or write it directly in the formula box. Click "Verify Formula" button to verify the formula and then click "OK".

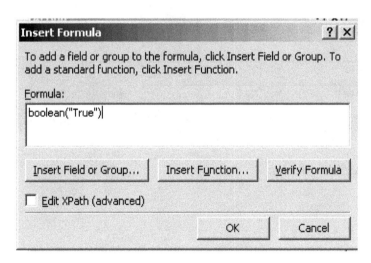

Figure 6.21: *Add Formula*

7. You need to add three more rules. Rules are shared between both option buttons. Rules you set for any of the option buttons work for both the buttons. Add second rule "Close Section 2". Set following condition:

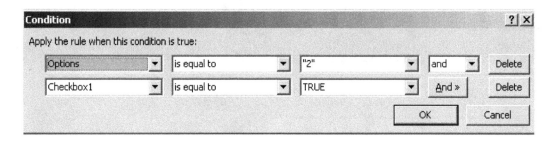

Figure 6.22: *Set condition for rule "Close Section 2"*

Add action for this rule. Select "Checkbox1" in "Field" and leave the value blank. This will uncheck the "Checkbox1".

8. Add third rule "Open Section 2" to open section 2. Set condition: Options is equal to "2" and add action: "Checkbox2" has value "boolean("True")". Use technique described above to add formula. Remember, typing formula manually will not set the boolean value and will be considered as plain text by InfoPath.

9. Add fourth rule "Close Section 1". Add following condition:

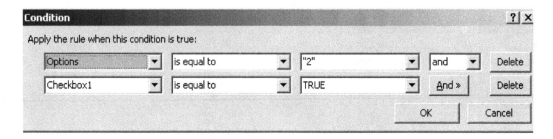

Figure 6.23: *Set condition for rule "Close Section 1"*

Add following action:

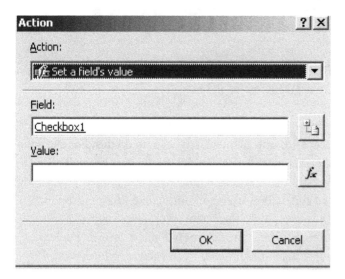

Figure 6.24: *Add action*

Select "Checkbox1" in "Field" and leave value blank. This will uncheck the "Checkbox1".
Remember sections are bound with these check boxes. Checking Checkbox1 will show section
1 and unchecking it will hide section 1. Similarly, checking Checkbox2 will show section 2 and
unchecking it will hide section 2.

That's it. The tip, in a nutshell, was that you should set the value of the checkbox to "blank" to
uncheck it. Setting it to "False" will not uncheck it.

Copying File Attachments from one section to another in InfoPath

If you have worked with InfoPath, you'll agree one has to come up with different techniques and tricks to implement solutions that are not available out-of-the-box.

In this section, I present a technique using which you can copy file attachments from one section to another. There are different scenarios in which you may want to do this. For example, consider a situation where you want to restrict users from deleting attachments once uploaded. Properties of file attachment control can only be set at design time and these properties once set cannot be changed dynamically. You can either allow users to insert/delete files or disallow them inserting or deleting files. Solution is to use two attachment controls and copy the content of one control to the other when user saves the form. One control will allow inserting/deleting files. The control will not allow inserting or deleting files and if you want to upload multiple files, then put the file attachment control in a repeating section. In this case, the read-only file attachment control should also be put in a repeating section. The source and destination data nodes hierarchy should be same otherwise copying of content will not work.

1. Start InfoPath 2007. Click "Data Source" in "Design Tasks".

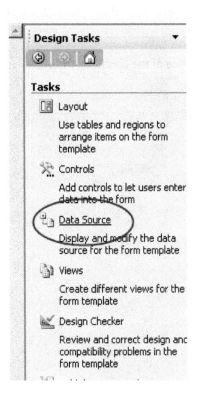

Figure 6.25: *Data Source (Design Tasks)*

2. Right-click "myFields" and select "Add..." from the menu.

Figure 6.26: *Add node*

3. Add name "group1" and from "Type" select "Group". Click OK.

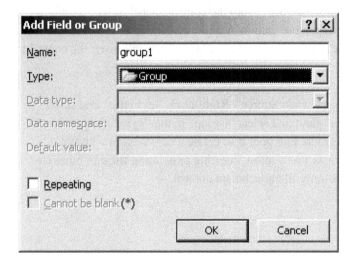

Figure 6.27: *Add group*

143

4. Right-click newly added group "group1" and select "Add..." from the menu. Enter "repGroup1" in the "Name" field and select "Group" from the "Type" field. Check "Repeating" checkbox at the bottom. This is important because this will be a repeating group. This repeating group will hold multiple file attachment controls.

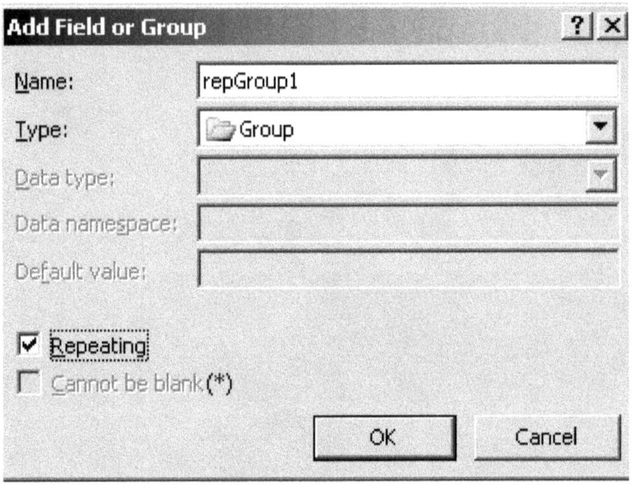

Figure 6.28: *Add repeating group*

5. Drag repeating group "repGroup1" and drop it on the form. This will insert a repeating section in the form.

6. Click "Design Tasks" and then click "Controls". From the controls panel, select "File Attachment" control and add it to the repeating section. Make sure the cursor is inside the repeating section and then double-click "File Attachment" control. This will insert the control in the repeating section.

7. Click "Design Tasks" again and select "Data Source". Right-click "myFields" and select "Add...". Enter "group2" in the "Name" field and select "Group" in the "Type" field. Click Ok. This will create a new non-repeating group. Our goal is to create a new section with file attachment control but in this case, we will now allow inserting or deleting files. In other words, it will be a read-only section with read-only file attachment control.

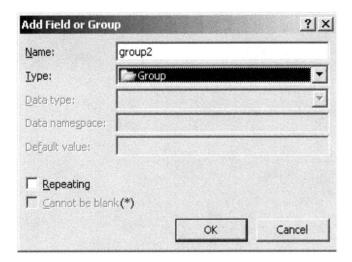

Figure 6.29: *Add destination group*

8. Right-click "repGroup1" and select "Reference..." from the menu. Select "group2" from the list and click "OK". This will add a repeating group and a data node in the "group2" node.

9. Drag "repGroup1" from "group2" and drop it on the form. Select repeating section from the menu that opens. This will add an empty repeating section on the form. Drag "field1" from "group2" and drop it inside the newly added repeating section. Now you have two identical repeating sections in the form. Advantage of using repeating section is, user can add as many file attachments as he or she likes.

10. Right-click second repeating section and select "Repeating Section Properties..." from the options menu. Uncheck "Allow users to insert and delete the sections". Click "OK".

11. Right-click second file attachment control and select "File Attachment Properties..." from the menu. Uncheck "Allow the user to browse, delete, and replace files" and click "OK".

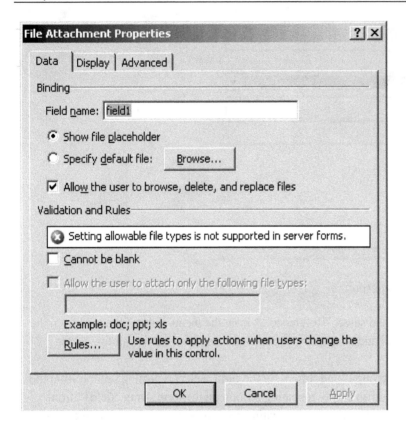

Figure 6.30: *Make file attachment read-only*

12. Add a button to the form (Design Tasks > Controls).

13. Select "Form Options" from the "Tools" menu.

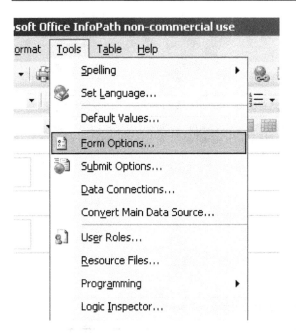

Figure 6.31: *Form Options*

14. Select "Programming" category. Select "C#" in the "Form template code language". Click "OK".

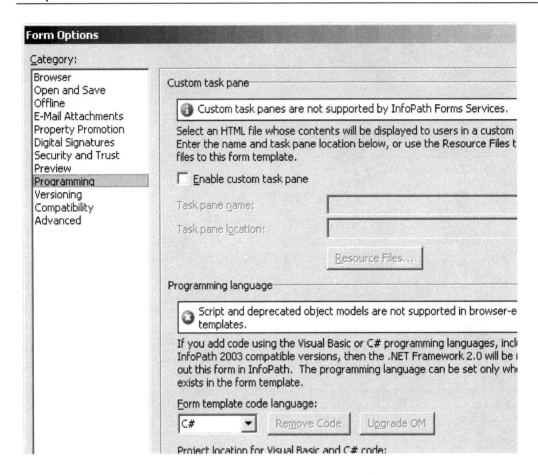

Figure 6.32: *Select programming language*

15. Double-click button and select "Edit Form Code". You will be prompted to save the form if you had not saved it already. Click "Ok". Give an appropriate name to your form. I kept the default name "Template1.xsn". This will create a new C# project for you. The location of the project, by default, will be as follows:

C:\Documents and Settings\Administrator\My Documents\InfoPath
Projects\Template11\Template1.csproj

Note, you can change this location by going to Tools > Form Options and then by selecting "Programming" from the categories. Change the location in the field called "Project location for VB and C# code". This field is located at the bottom.

16. Copy following code to the project:

```
private void CopyAttachments()

{

string srcXPath = "/my:myFields/my:group1";

string destXPath = "/my:myFields/my:group2";

string srcNodeXPath = "/my:myFields/my:group1/repGroup1";

XPathNavigator source = this.CreateNavigator().SelectSingleNode(srcXPath,
this.NamespaceManager);

XPathNavigator dest = this.CreateNavigator().SelectSingleNode(destXPath,
this.NamespaceManager);

if (dest.MoveToAttribute("nil", "http://www.w3.org/2001/XMLSchema-instance"))

dest.DeleteSelf();

if (source.InnerXml.Contains("xsi:nil="))

{

//Do nothing

}

else

{

if (dest.InnerXml.Contains("xsi:nil="))

{
```

```
dest.InnerXml = source.InnerXml;

}

else

{

dest.InnerXml += source.InnerXml;

}

//clear source files

XPathNavigator srcFiles = this.CreateNavigator().SelectSingleNode(srcNodeXPath,
this.NamespaceManager);

if (IsGridDirty(srcNodeXPath))

{

XPathNodeIterator Node_To_Be_Deleted = this.CreateNavigator().Select(srcNodeXPath,
NamespaceManager);

string groupResults = srcNodeXPath;

XPathNavigator firstItem;

XPathNavigator lastItem;

if (Node_To_Be_Deleted.Count > 1)

{

firstItem = srcFiles.SelectSingleNode(groupResults + "[1]", NamespaceManager);

lastItem = srcFiles.SelectSingleNode(groupResults + "[position()=last()]",
NamespaceManager);
```

```
firstItem.DeleteRange(lastItem);

//clean up local variables

lastItem = null;

firstItem = null;

}

else if (Node_To_Be_Deleted.Count == 1)

{

firstItem = srcFiles.SelectSingleNode(groupResults + "[1]", NamespaceManager);

firstItem.DeleteSelf();

}

//clean up

Node_To_Be_Deleted = null;

}

//clean up

srcFiles = null;

}

}

private bool IsGridDirty(string ControlName)

{

try
```

```
{
```

//This function checks whether the Results node has any items or not, returns true if the number of items is greater than 0.

```
XPathNavigator _DOM = this.MainDataSource.CreateNavigator();

XPathNodeIterator nodes = _DOM.Select(ControlName, this.NamespaceManager);

XPathNavigator nodesNavigator = nodes.Current;

XPathNodeIterator nodesText = nodesNavigator.SelectDescendants(XPathNodeType.Text,
false);

int counter = 0;

while (nodesText.MoveNext())

{

if (nodesText.Current.NodeType == XPathNodeType.Text)

{
```

//if (nodesText.Current.Name == "Section5_Selected" && (nodesText.Current.Value == "true" || nodesText.Current.Value == "false" || nodesText.Current.Value == "" || nodesText.Current.Value == "blank"))

```
//{

counter += 1;

//}

}

}
```

//clean up

```
nodesText = null;

nodesNavigator = null;

nodes = null;

_DOM = null;

//return count

if (counter > 0)

{

return true;

}

else

{

return false;

}

}

catch (Exception ex)

{

return false;

}

}
```

Listing 6.7: *Complete code*

Check these lines:

string srcXPath = "/my:myFields/my:group1";

string destXPath = "/my:myFields/my:group2";

string srcNodeXPath = "/my:myFields/my:group1/repGroup1";

Paths should be correct. srcXPath contains the xPath of the source group, that is, group1. destXPath contains the xPath for the destination group, that is, group2. srcNodeXPath contains the xPath of first repeating group.

16. Call "CopyAttachments()" in the button's click:

```
public void CTRL5_5_Clicked(object sender, ClickedEventArgs e)
{
    CopyAttachments();
}
```

Listing 6.8: Call CopyAttachments

17. Save the project, compile it and publish the form. Add attachments to the first repeating section and click the button. The files will be copied to the second repeating section and cleared from the first repeating section. Now users cannot delete files from the second repeating section. Usually this function is called when the form is submitted because before the form is saved or submitted, user can change the files.

Managing older versions of InfoPath forms

Here is a small tip to manage older versions of InfoPath forms. This is a very simple tip and the solution is available out-of-the-box but unfortunately, InfoPath developers usually ignore this built-in feature and face problems after deploying the updated forms. You may have noticed that you get "Schema validation errors found" when opening an updated form. In fact, the form fails to open and it is difficult to locate the data sources that cause the problem. This question is asked frequently in the forums where users ask for solutions to fix the problem. Some users manually upgrade the XML of existing forms to make them compatible with the new template. In the "Form Options", inside "Versioning" category, there is an option to manage version upgrades.

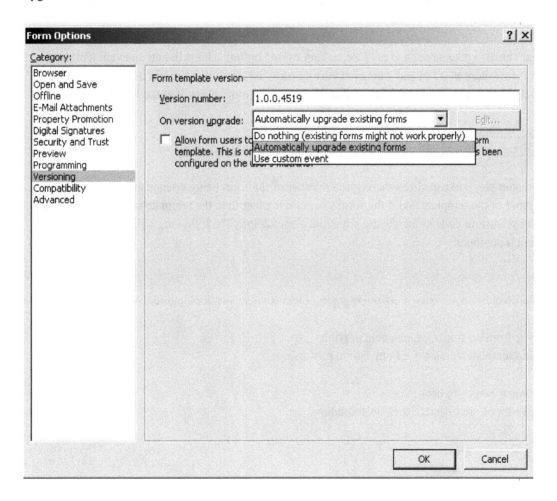

Figure 6.33: *Form Options*

The drop down has three options:

> Do nothing (existing forms might not work properly)
> Automatically upgrade existing forms
> Use custom event

By default, the first option "Do nothing ..." is selected. Select the second option "Automatically upgrade existing forms" and save changes. Publish your form. This will automatically upgrade the existing forms and you won't have to update their XML manually which can be quite cumbersome if the library contains hundreds or thousands of forms which is a common scenario in big companies. Some times, it is necessary to keep the existing forms as they are and upgrade them manually if need be but that is rare.

User can also take advantage of "Use custom event" option. This will add an event handler to the form where you can add your own custom code but this will be useful only if you know what changes you had made in the form. You can read more about it at the following link:

http://msdn.microsoft.com/en-us/library/microsoft.office.infopath.formevents.versionupgrade.aspx

For example, you can check the version number of the form being opened and the version number of the template and if the form's version is older than the template's version then you can use custom code to handle the situation. For example, the following will give you the version numbers:

```
public void FormEvents_VersionUpgrade(object sender, VersionUpgradeEventArgs e)
{
string formVersion = e.DocumentVersion;
string templateVersion = e.FormTemplateVersion;

//comparison code here
//if versions are different then do something

}
```

Listing 6.9: *VersionUpgrade*

Another option is to add checks in the form using code. Suppose you added a new data source in the form. This data source will not be available in the forms based on the older template. You can check for the existence of the data source/node programmatically and handle business logic accordingly. For example, here is some sample code:

```
XPathNavigator node =
this.CreateNavigator().SelectSingleNode("/my:myFields/my:newNode",
this.NamespaceManager);
if (node != null) //if this node exists
{
  //Logic 1
}
else
{
  //Logic 2
}

node = null;
```

Listing 6.10: *Business logic*

You simplly check the existence of the data source by comparing it to "null". If it's not null (node exists), run new logic for the new form else skip the new logic to keep the old forms intact.

Creating a filtered column in InfoPath (data from a SharePoint list)

Scenario: You have a list in SharePoint that contains user data (profile including name, phone, etc). You have an InfoPath form that has a text box to enter a user ID and a button to show record against the User ID entered in the text box.

Being a developer, a programmatic solution is very easy for me. With a few lines of code I can extract filtered data from a SharePoint list. What about those who are not SharePoint programmers! This tip will give you an easy solution.

A. Add a new data connection in your form.

1. Click "Manage Data Connections" in "Design Tasks". This will open a "Data Connections" box.

2. Click the "Add" button.

3. Select "Create a new connection to" option and then select "Receive data" option. Click "Next".

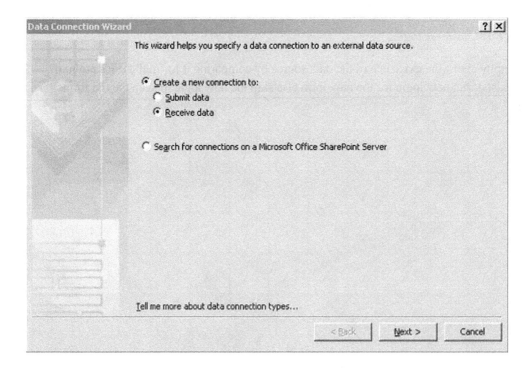

Figure 6.34: *Receive connection*

4. Select "SharePoint library or list" and click "Next".

5. Enter the URL of the list that will be used to fetch data from. Click "Next".

6. Select list from the available lists and libraries and click "Next".

7. Select the fields that you want to show in the form and click "Next". If you intend to use the form in Offline mode (that is when you are not connected to the SharePoint), then select the option "Store a copy of the data in the form template" otherwise do nothing and click "Next".

8. Enter a name for this new data connection and select "Automatically retrieve data when form is opened" and click "Finish".

9. Click "Close".

B. Display data in your form. Suppose you want to show a single field/column in your form. Follow the instructions below to show a single field.

1. Add a data source (type: string).

2. Right click the new data source and select "Properties".

3. "Data" tab is selected by default when your open the control's properties. Click the function button (fx) that is located on the right side of the "Value" field.

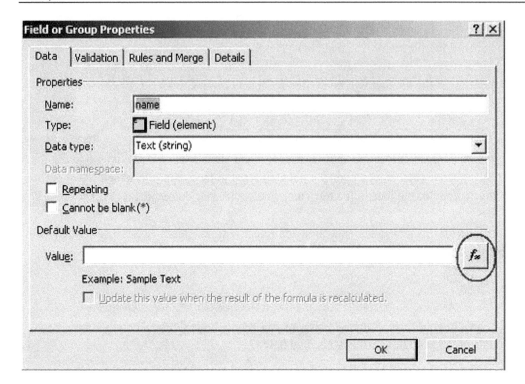

Figure 6.35: *Field or group properties*

4. Click "Insert Field or Group…" button.

5. Select the data connection that you created in the first step from the "Data Source" drop down.

6. Expand nodes unless you can see all field/column names. Select the column name that you want to show in your form. As I said earlier, we are assuming that we are retrieving user profile data from a SharePoint list and this data will be filtered by a value passed from the InfoPath form. As I mentioned in the scenario above, there is a field that will contain a User ID entered by the user. So after you select the value that you want to show on your form, click the "Filter Data…" button. This button remains disabled unless you select a field.

7. Click "Add" button.

8. There will be three drop down boxes on the form. The first drop down will have the column names retrieved from the SharePoint list and by default the column name you selected in the previous step will be selected in the drop down. The second drop down contains the filter conditions. Keep the default condition selected, that is, "is equal to". In the third drop down, Select "Type text …" if you want to hard code the user ID against which you want to show the

160

data. If you want to keep it dynamic then select "Select a field or group...".

9. From the "Data Source" drop down, select the main data source and then select the field name that corresponds to the "User ID" text box on your form. Click "Ok" and then again click "Ok". Click "Ok" thrice more to close open boxes and then click "Ok" once more to close the main properties box.

10. Drag and drop the data source to your form. Save the form and run it to view the preview. (Hint: If this is a web enabled form, make sure to set the postback settings of the control that will show data to "Always".)

Repeat the steps above for each new field added to your form to show the SharePoint list column data.

Submitting InfoPath data to a SharePoint list

InfoPath data can be stored anywhere, in any database, even in a text file. Sometimes, there is a need to store the data somewhere else other than the library itself. The form that is submitted and saved in Forms library is an XML form and contains data. This data can also be submitted to other locations when user clicks the submit button. In this article, we will see how we can store this data in a SharePoint list.

1. Create a custom list in SharePoint with the following fields:

a. FirstName
b. LastName
c. Address
d. Zip
e. City
f. State
g. Country
h. Phone
i. Fax
j. Web

Data type for all the fields will be "Single line of Text".

2. Open "user registration" form in editor.

3. Open VSTA

4. Add reference to "Microsoft.SharePoint.DLL".

There are some steps that you need to take before adding the real code. We covered these steps in previous articles but just in case, if you landed directly on this page, here are the steps again:

5. Add a event handler in "InternalStartup()" function

```
EventManager.FormEvents.Loading += new LoadingEventHandler(FormEvents_Loading);
```

Listing 6.11: *Add event handler*

6. Add the following in the class:

```
private string LibLocation

{

get

{

return (string)FormState["LibLocation"];

}

set

{

FormState["LibLocation"] = value;

}

}

private string Location

{

get

{

return (string)FormState["Location"];

}

set

{
```

```
FormState["Location"] = value;

}

}
```

Listing 6.12: *Add code*

7. Add following code in the FormEvents_Loading():

```
//Edit mode

if (e.InputParameters.ContainsKey("XmlLocation"))

{

Location = e.InputParameters["Source"].ToString();

Location = Location.Substring(0, Location.IndexOf("/", 8));

LibLocation = Location + e.InputParameters["XmlLocation"].ToString();

}
else

{

//New mode

LibLocation = e.InputParameters["SaveLocation"].ToString();

}
```

Listing 6.13: *Add code in form's loading event*

This code defines location for the form submission, that is, the URL where the form would be submitted.

8. Add following code in the "Submit_Clicked()":

```
XPathNavigator fname =
this.CreateNavigator().SelectSingleNode("/my:myFields/my:FirstName",
this.NamespaceManager);
XPathNavigator lname =
this.CreateNavigator().SelectSingleNode("/my:myFields/my:LastName",
this.NamespaceManager);
XPathNavigator address =
this.CreateNavigator().SelectSingleNode("/my:myFields/my:Address",
this.NamespaceManager);
XPathNavigator zip = this.CreateNavigator().SelectSingleNode("/my:myFields/my:Zip",
this.NamespaceManager);
XPathNavigator city = this.CreateNavigator().SelectSingleNode("/my:myFields/my:City",
this.NamespaceManager);
XPathNavigator state =
this.CreateNavigator().SelectSingleNode("/my:myFields/my:State",
this.NamespaceManager);
XPathNavigator country =
this.CreateNavigator().SelectSingleNode("/my:myFields/my:Country",
this.NamespaceManager);
XPathNavigator phone =
this.CreateNavigator().SelectSingleNode("/my:myFields/my:Phone",
this.NamespaceManager);
XPathNavigator fax = this.CreateNavigator().SelectSingleNode("/my:myFields/my:Fax",
this.NamespaceManager);
XPathNavigator web = this.CreateNavigator().SelectSingleNode("/my:myFields/my:Web",
this.NamespaceManager);

SPWeb webroot = null;
try
{
webroot = SPContext.Current.Web;
SPSecurity.RunWithElevatedPrivileges(delegate()
{
using (SPSite site = new SPSite(webroot.Site.ID))
```

```
{
using (SPWeb localweb = site.OpenWeb(webroot.ID))
{
SPList list = localweb.Lists["User List"];
SPListItem listItem = list.Items.Add();
localweb.AllowUnsafeUpdates = true;
listItem["Title"] = fname.Value.ToString();
listItem["FirstName"] = fname.Value.ToString();
listItem["LastName"] = lname.Value.ToString();
listItem["Address"] = address.Value.ToString();
listItem["Zip"] = zip.Value.ToString();
listItem["City"] = city.Value.ToString();
listItem["State"] = state.Value.ToString();
listItem["Country"] = country.Value.ToString();
listItem["Phone"] = phone.Value.ToString();
listItem["Fax"] = fax.Value.ToString();
listItem["Web"] = web.Value.ToString();
listItem.Update();
localweb.AllowUnsafeUpdates = false;
}
}
});

FileSubmitConnection SubmitConnection =
(FileSubmitConnection)this.DataConnections["Main submit"];
SubmitConnection.FolderUrl = LibLocation.Substring(0, LibLocation.LastIndexOf("/"));

SubmitConnection.Execute();
```

Listing 6.14: *Submit code*

This code will get data from the form and submit it to the SharePoint list. First we create XPathNavigator objects for each of the form fields. We read value from each field. Inserting data into a SharePoint list seems to be simple but there are some caveats that you need to be aware of. "SPWeb webroot = null" should be declared outside the try ... catch block. You cannot define it inside the "using" statement. It will throw an error. It is important to use "RunWithElevatedPrivileges" to avoid the permissions exception. If you don't declare "webroot" object outside the try ... catch block, you get an "Operation is not valid due to the current state of the object." error. In the end, define an object of "FileSubmitConnection" type and use the "Execute()" method to submit the form to the library.

Download completed InfoPath form and application code (ZIP format):

http://walisystems.com/articles/SPS/addtolist/add_to_list.zip

Creating web enabled InfoPath forms

In this section, you will learn how to create web enabled InfoPath forms. InfoPath is an information gathering tool and is used to create XML forms. People have always been trying to come up with a standard for creating electronic forms. Before InfoPath, companies created electronic forms in different formats. InfoPath has helped companies to adhere to a standard. Coding XML manually may not be an interesting job but creating XML forms with InfoPath has really made this job quite easier.

All clients must have InfoPath installed on their machines in order to open the forms. It could be a problem for smaller companies to provide InfoPath client to all the users. What can be the solution then? Solution is to create web enabled forms that can be opened in web browser without having to install InfoPath client on user machines.

Following is a step-by-step guide that will show you how to create and deploy a web enabled form:

1. Open InfoPath (Start > All Programs > Microsoft Office > Microsoft Office InfoPath 2007)

2. On the "Getting Started" screen, under "Design a form", click "Design a form template".

3. On the "Design a form template" screen, select "Form Template" and check the checkbox "Enable browser-compatible features only" at the bottom. Make sure it's based on a "Blank" template.

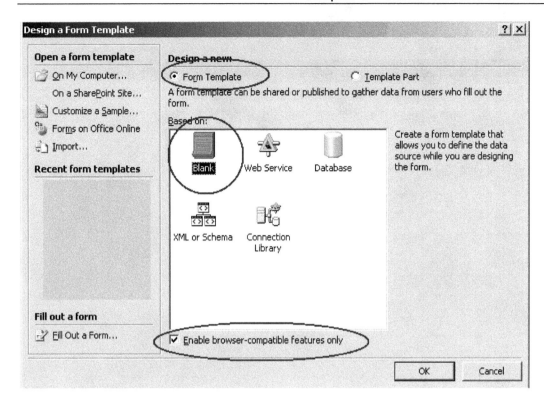

Figure 6.36: *Design a form template*

4. From the "Format" menu, select "Layout...".

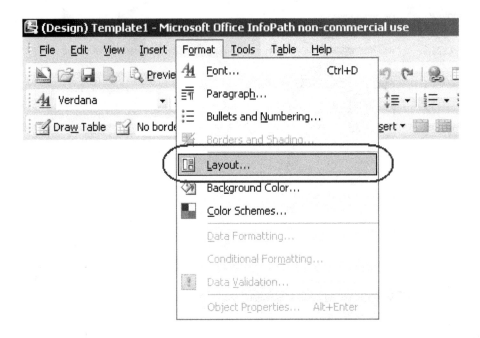

Figure 6.37: *Design layout*

5. From the "Layout" table on the right side, select "Table with Title". This will insert a table with a header. You can change the color theme by selecting a color scheme from the "Format > Color Schemes..." menu.

6. Change the header to "User Registration".

7. Click in the area "Click to add form content". Right-click the area and select "Split Cells..." from the menu. Split the column into two. Add following labels in the left column. Add each label in a new row:

- First Name
- Last Name
- Address
- Zip
- City
- State
- Country
- Phone
- Fax

170

- Web

8. In the right column, add text boxes against each label. Click "Design Tasks" from the table on the right side.

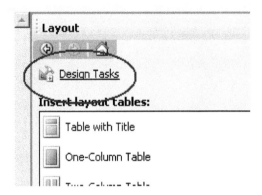

Figure 6.38: *Layout (Design Tasks)*

9. Click "Controls" in the design tasks and then select "Text Box" from the "Standard" controls section. Drag text box into the first row, second column and rename it to "FirstName". To rename, right click the text box and select "Text Box Properties" and change the field name. Do the same for all other fields, add text boxes and rename them as following:

- LastName
- Address
- Zip
- City
- State
- Country
- Phone
- Fax
- Web

Tip: Use font "Verdana" and size "8.5".

10. Add two buttons at the bottom and rename them to "Submit" and "Close". The completed form will look like the following:

User Registration	
First Name	
Last Name	
Address	
Zip	
City	
State	
Country	
Phone	
Fax	
Web	
	Submit Close

Figure 6.39: *User Registration Form*

11. From "Tools" menu, select "Form Options..."

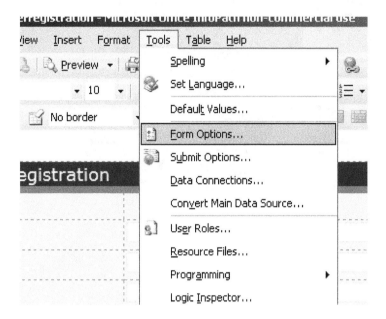

Figure 6.40: *Form Options*

12. Make sure "Browser" is selected in the "Category" and uncheck the following toolbar options:

- Show toolbar at top of form
- Show toolbar at bottom of form

13. Select "Security and Trust" in "Category". Uncheck "Automatically determine security level (recommended)" checkbox. Select "Full Trust (the form has access to files and settings on the computer)" option button.

14. Select "Programming" category. Select C# as the programming language and select a location to save the code.

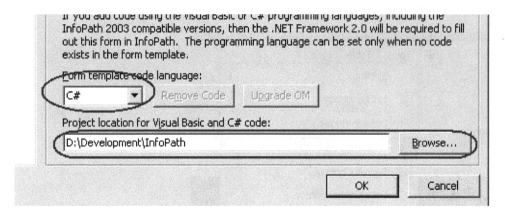

Figure 6.41: *Select programming language*

15. Select "Compatibility" category. Check the option "Design a form template that can be opened in a browser or InfoPath". Add a URL in the text box provided below. This will be the URL of the forms services web service. The URL will be:

http://server/_vti_bin/FormsServices.asmx

Note: server name in the URL above will be different for you.

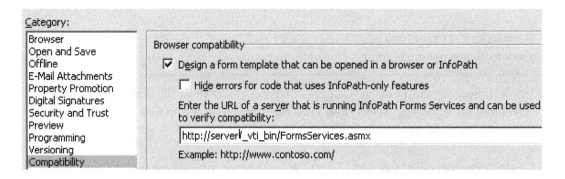

Figure 6.42: *Browser compatibility*

16. Click OK to save all these changes.

17. Ok, it's time to publish the form. Select "Publish..." from the "File" menu.

18. Select first option "To a SharePoint server with or without InfoPath Forms Services" in the publishing wizard.

19. Provide a URL where this form will be published. This will be location on your SharePoint server. You can select the root path, for example, http://server and click "Next".

20. Check the option "Enable the form to be filled out by using a browser" and click "Next".

21. Click "Browse" button and select a location on your hard disk where this template will be saved. Give your template a name. I named it "userregistrationtpl.xsn". Click "Next".

22. Click "Add" button to add columns that you want to appear on your SharePoint Forms Library. For example, Click "Add" and then select "FirstName" from the columns. Select "(None: Create new column in this library)" option from the "Site column group:" drop down. A column name "First Name" will automatically be entered in the "Column name". You can change it to your liking. Add as many columns as you like and click "OK" to save. Click "Next" then click "Publish" and finally click "Close" to close the wizard.

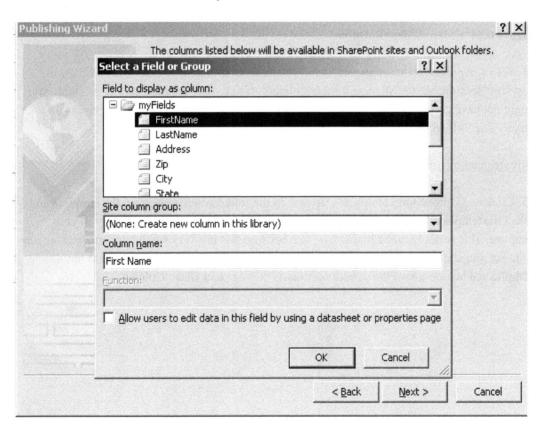

Figure 6.43: *Publishing wizard*

Uploading the published web form

23. There are two ways to upload the published web form to SharePoint: Using the interface provided by SharePoint and using the command line tool stsadm.exe. I will show you both methods. First, let's try the first method, that is, using the SharePoint admin interface. Open "SharePoint Central Administration" site by selecting Start > All Programs > Microsoft Office Server > SharePoint 3.0 Central Administration.

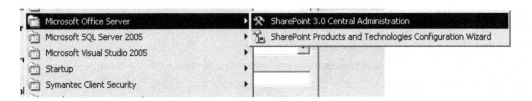

Figure 6.44: *Central Administration*

24. Select "Application Management" from "Central Administration". In "InfoPath Forms Services" section, select "Manage form templates". If you don't see this seciton, probably you might not have configured the forms services on your server. Enable "Forms Services" on your server. The following technet article has the details:

http://technet.microsoft.com/en-us/library/cc262263.aspx

25. Click on "Upload form template". Browse to the folder where you saved the template and select the template file. Click the "Verify" button to make sure there are no errors in your template. This is not required in this template because this is a very small template without any code but you should always verify the template before uploading if it has code and has a complicated layout. Leave the default options as they are and click "Upload".

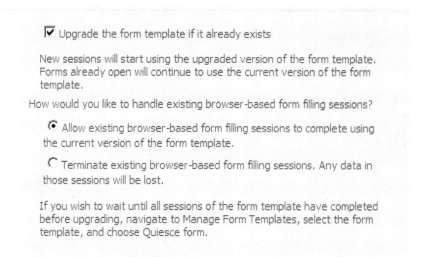

Figure 6.45: *Upgrade the form template*

26. You will see a message after the form has been uploaded. Click Ok. You will be shown the list of uploaded forms. Select the form you just uploaded. Move the mouse over the form name. Click the down arrow. Select "Activate to a Site Collection".

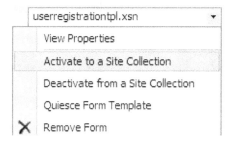

Figure 6.46: *Activate to a Site Collection*

27. Change the site collection in the "Site Collection" drop down. If you only have one site collection then you don't need to worry about it. If you have multiple site collections, then select the one where you want to activate the template. Click the down arrow and then click "Change Site Collection". Change the web application in the "Web Application" drop down. Again if you have only one web application or the web application of your choice is already selected then leave it as it is. You can select a site from the left side that shows the sites' links. By default, root "/" is selected. Click OK. Click OK again to activate the template on the site collection you selected.

177

Select Site Collection

URL Search [   ] 🔍

URL

/

/sites/sc1

/sites/test

Figure 6.47: *Select Site Collection*

Preparing the Forms Library

28. Open a SharePoint site. If you have already created a Forms library then you just need to configure it for the InfoPath template otherwise, create a new Forms Library. Open "Form Library Settings".

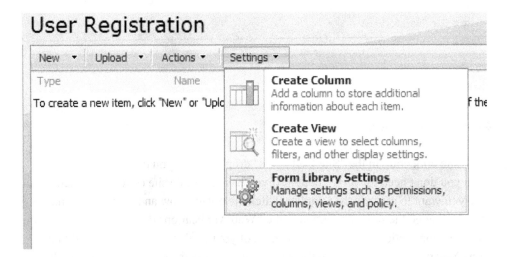

Figure 6.48: *Form Library Settings*

29. Go to "Advanced Settings". Set "Allow management of content types?" to "Yes". Set

"Opening browser-enabled documents" to "Display as a Web page". In the "Folders" section, set "Display "New Folder" command on the New menu?" to "No". Set the last option "Allow items from this form library to appear in search results?" to "Yes". Click OK.

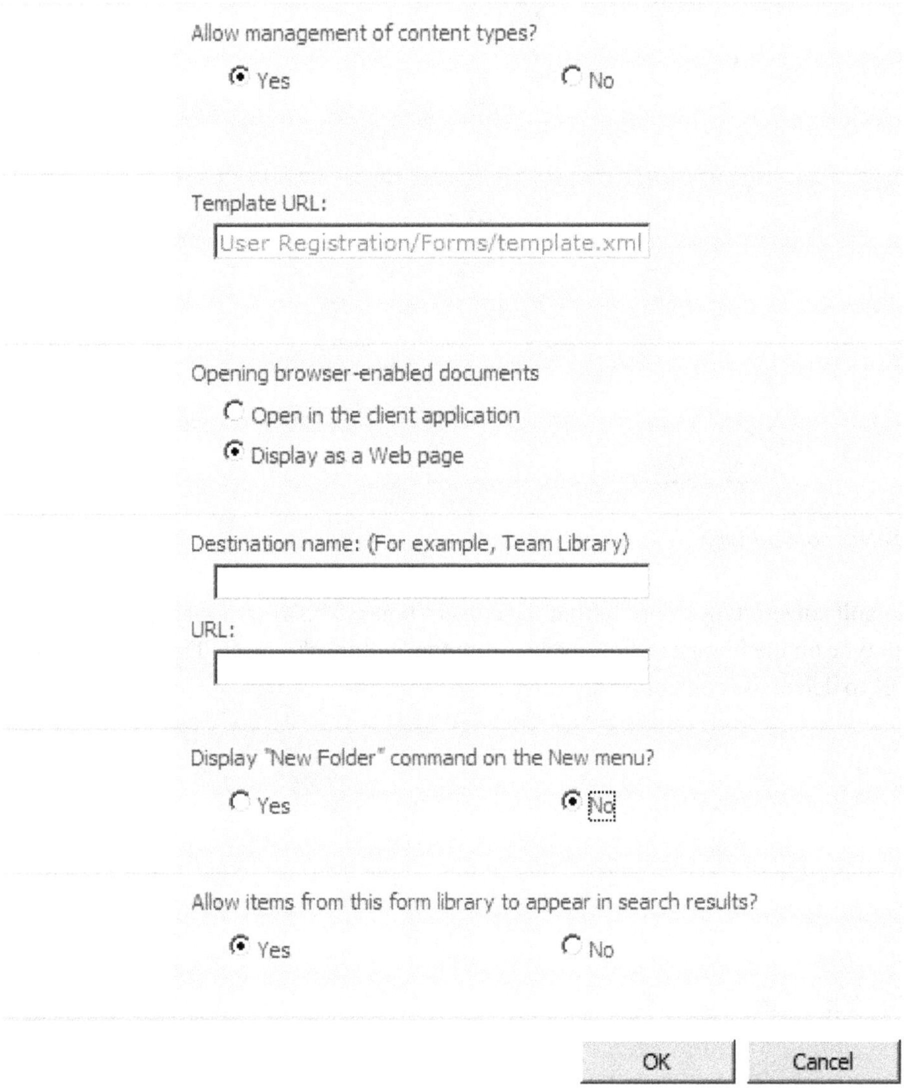

Allow management of content types?

    ⦿ Yes   ○ No

Template URL:

User Registration/Forms/template.xml

Opening browser-enabled documents

    ○ Open in the client application
    ⦿ Display as a Web page

Destination name: (For example, Team Library)

URL:

Display "New Folder" command on the New menu?

    ○ Yes   ⦿ No

Allow items from this form library to appear in search results?

    ⦿ Yes   ○ No

| OK | Cancel |

Figure 6.49: *Library settings*

30. In the library settings' "Content Types" section, click "Add from existing site content types". Select the template that you uploaded from the list of available site content types and click the "Add >" button and click Ok.

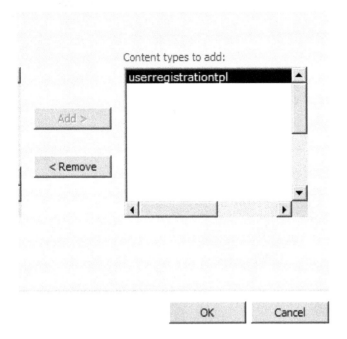

Figure 6.50: *Select content type*

Remove the default content type "Form" from the content types. This is optional. Click the "Form" content type on the library settings page. From the "Settings", select "Delete this content type". Click OK to delete the content type.

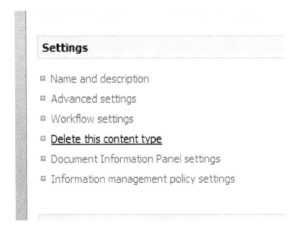

Figure 6.51: *Delete existing (forms) content type*

31. Go back to the library and click the "New" button. It will open the form template. That's it.

180

You have just published a web enabled InfoPath form. The form doesn't do anything but the article was meant to show you the publishing process. In the next article we will make this form functional.

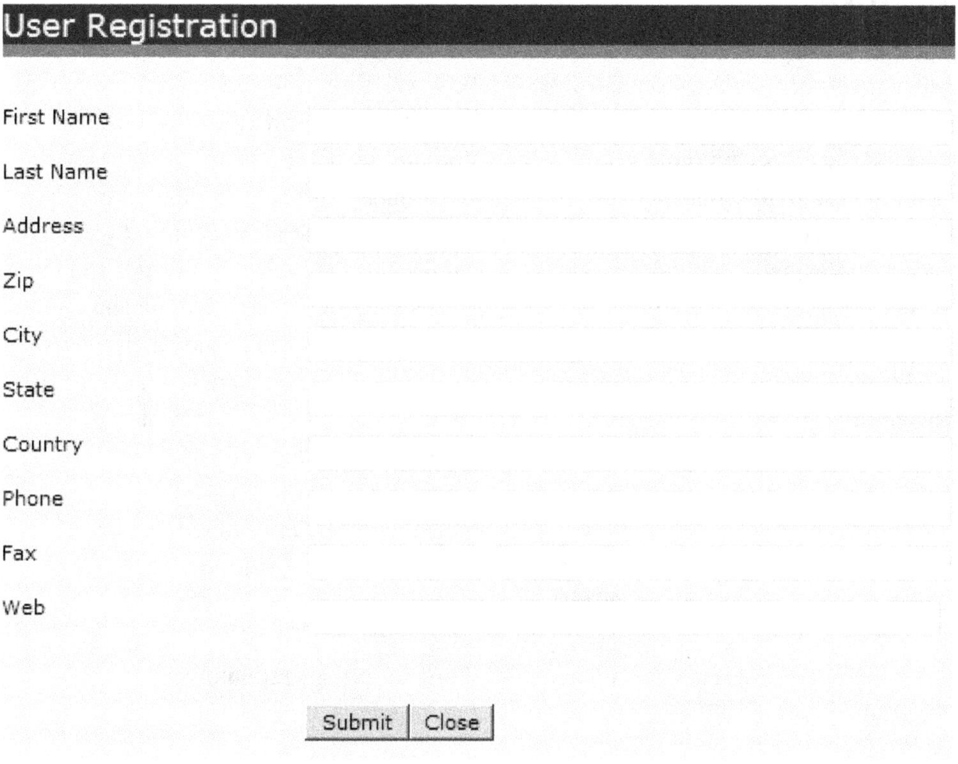

User Registration

First Name

Last Name

Address

Zip

City

State

Country

Phone

Fax

Web

Submit | Close

Figure 6.52: *Completed User Registration Form*

Download completed template:

http://walisystems.com/articles/SPS/webinfopath/userregistrationtpl.xsn

Publishing InfoPath web form using stsadm command line utility

In this section, you will see how to publish an InfoPath web form using an stsadm command line utility. In previous section "Creating Web Enabled InfoPath Form", you saw how to publish the form using SharePoint Central Administration site, that is, using the web interface. In large organizations that have multiple departments and servers running multiple applications at a time, deploying forms manually may not be a good idea because it will never be a one time deployment. In big organzations, the applications are released in steps and there is version control. Also, there are bug fixes and there is a need for an easy deployment method that does not involve developer interaction. Administrators can create batch files to upload and deploy the forms. Stsadm.exe utility comes in handy when there is a need for such tasks. This utility does a lot of other things which we won't discuss here as they are not relevant but some commands that are important will be discussed in detail.

Ok, the form is ready. We already deployed it using the interface. Now we will deploy it using the command line tool. The first command that we will look at is following:

```
stsadm.exe -o VerifyFormTemplate -filename "C:\Forms\userregistrationtpl.xsn"
```

Listing 6.15: *VerifyFormTemplate*

The operation that we use in this command is "VerifyFormTemplate". It verifies that the template is free of errors. In case there are errors, they will be displayed in the console window. The parameter we used is "filename". This is the complete file path on your disk. It is important that you run this command before uploading the form on the server. There are some errors that cannot be caught during the upload process. Your template won't work even if the uploading is successful. The only way to make sure that there are no errors in your form are to run this command.

You can also use the "Design Checker" in InfoPath to check for errors.

Figure 6.53: *Design Checker*

You can also use "Logic Inspector" to find errors in your logic, rules, etc but there is no guarantee that your form will be free of errors even after running these tools. Yes, I agree this does not make sense. There should be a way to test the form for errors before handing it over to the Administrator but that's the way InfoPath works. The only way to make sure that form template is free of errors is to use the "VerifyFormTemplate" operation with stsadm.exe command.

The second command is for uploading the template to the server:

```
stsadm.exe -o UploadFormTemplate -filename "C:\Forms\userregistrationtpl.xsn"
```

Listing 6.16: *UploadFormTemplate*

We use "UploadFormTemplate" operation to upload the form. The "filename" parameter contains the full path of the file on your disk.

The third command is for activating the template on the server. The operation that we use is "ActivateFormTemplate" and we pass two parameters. The first one is "URL" which is the site collection URL where you want to activate the template. The second parameter is "filename" which is the full path of the template on the disk.

```
stsadm.exe -o ActivateFormTemplate -url "http://server" -filename
"C:\Forms\userregistrationtpl.xsn"
```

Listing 6.17: *ActivateFormTemplate*

There is another way of activating the form on the site. You have seen two methods already. The third one is through the interface but not central administration this time. Just go to the SharePoint root site. Go to :"Site Settings". Under "Site Collection Administration" you will find a link "Site collection features". Click it. Find your template in the list. You will see "Activate" button in front of the template name. Click it to activate the template. Similarly to deactivate it, click the "Deactivate" button (Activate will turn into Deactivate once the form is activated). The status is shown next to the button.

Ok, now you have activated the form. There should be a way to deactivate and remove the form from the server. The command to deactivate the form on the server is as following:

```
stsadm.exe -o DeactivateFormTemplate -url "http://server" -filename
"C:\Forms\userregistrationtpl.xsn"
```

Listing 6.18: *DeactivateFormTemplate*

This command will deactivate the template. The parameters are "URL" and the "Filename".

To remove the form from the server, use following command:

```
stsadm.exe -o RemoveFormTemplate -filename "C:\Forms\userregistrationtpl.xsn"
```

Listing 6.19: *RemoveFormTemplate*

This will remove the template from the server. The only parameter is "filename".

You will get an error if the following service is not running on the server:

Windows SharePoint Services Administration

Go to Control Panel and Service and start this service if it's not already started. You can also

184

use another stsadm command to run the administrative service jobs in which the Windows SharePoint Services Administration (SPAdmin) service has been disabled. The command is:

```
stsadm -o execadmsvcjobs
```

Listing 6.20: *stsadm utility*

This will execute the pending jobs on the server. Sometimes, you will get the following error.

The solution-deployment-jobxx.wsp-0 job completed successfully, but could not be properly cleaned up. This job may execute again on this server. Operation completed successfully.

Ignore the error. The job has been run.

Create a batch file and add all the commands shown above to automate the deployment process. If the form is already deployed and you just want to upgrade the template, use the following command:

```
stsadm.exe -o UpgradeFormTemplate -filename "C:\Forms\userregistrationtpl.xsn"
```

Listing 6.21: *UpgradeFormTemplate*

This will upgrade the template. If you made changes to the promoted fields, for example, promoted new fields or demoted some of the already promoted fields, you will have to reactivate the template on the server for the changes to take effect.

Programming InfoPath Web Forms

You have seen how to create a web enabled InfoPath form. You have also seen techniques to publish the form. What Next? How to program a web form! We will add code to the form that we created in one of the previous sections. We added two buttons. The buttons did not do anything. We will add the "Submit" functionality. Open the form in InfoPath editor.

1. Right click the "Submit" button and select "Button Properties".

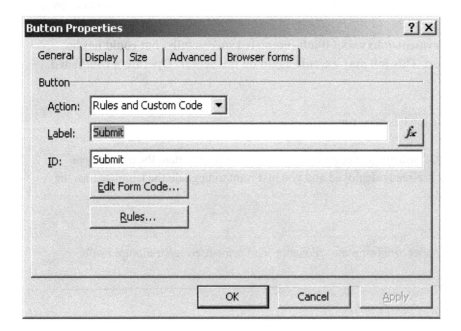

Figure 6.54: *Button properties*

2. In the "Action" drop down, select "Submit" and then click "Submit Options" button (It will appear after you select "Submit" in Action drop down).

3. Check "Allow users to submit this form" option. From the drop down that gets enabled, select "SharePoint document library".

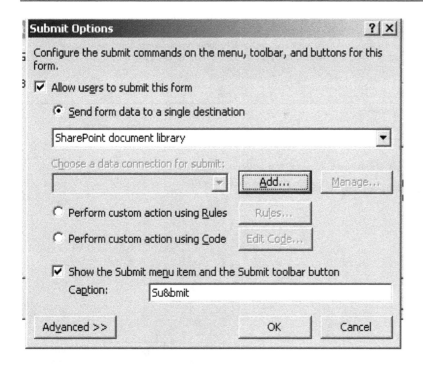

Figure 6.55: *Submit options*

There will be an "Add" button underneath the drop down. Click it to add a data connection.

4. Add URL of the forms library in the "Document Library" box.

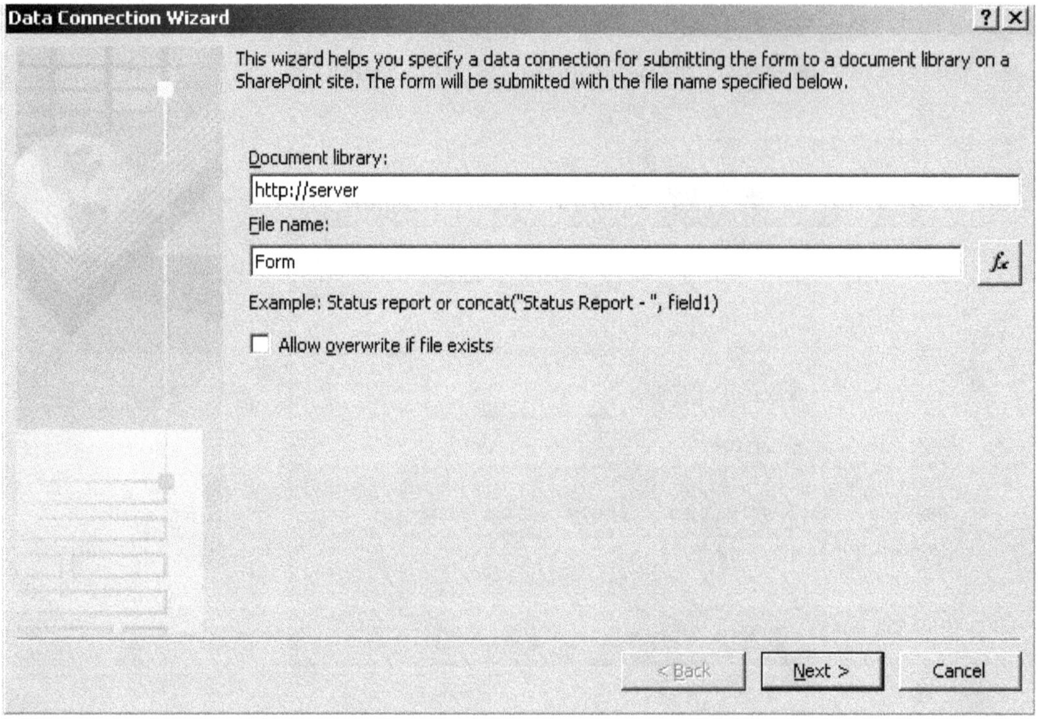

Figure 6.56: *Data connection wizard*

By default, the name of the saved XML forms will be "Form". This will pose a problem because only form with this name will be saved. For new forms that you will try to save will give you an error because of the name conflict. The solution is to check the "Allow overwrite if file exists" option but will that solve the problem. Not necessarily! That will work if you want to save only one form in the library but for multiple forms, each form must have a unique name. Click the "fx" button. This will open the "Insert Formula" wizard.

5. Click "Inert Function" button.

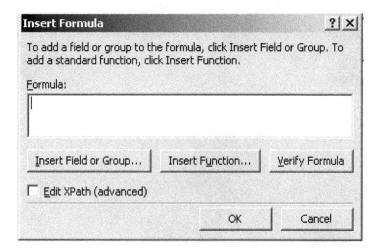

Figure 6.57: *Insert formula*

6. From the "Functions", select "concat" function and click OK.

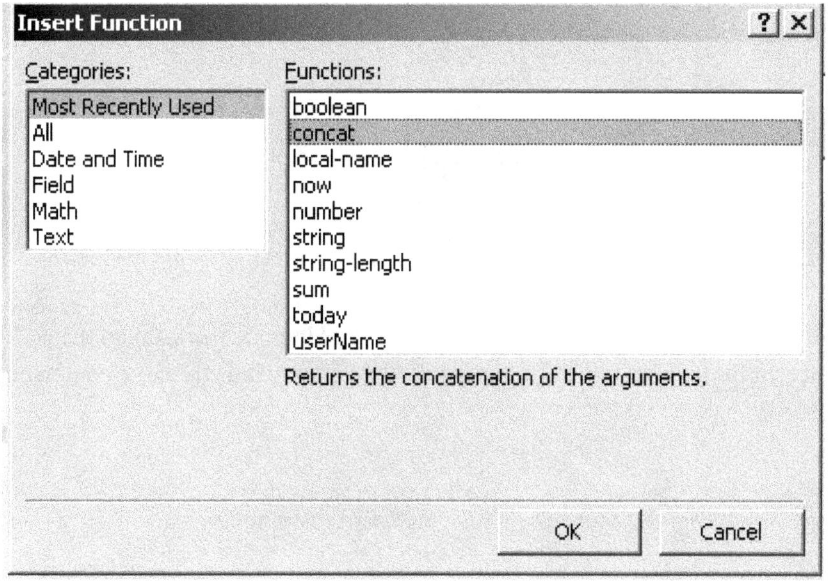

Figure 6.58: *Insert function*

7. Remove the first two parameters from the function and add "Form-" in place of them. Double-click the third parameter "double click to insert field" to insert a field. It will open the list of fields available in the form. Select "LastName". Your form will now be named as "Form-

189

" plus the last name of the user taken from the form. For example, if the last name of the user is "Doe", the form name will be "Form-Doe". Click OK to save the settings. Click "Next" to move to the next step.

8. Enter a name for this data connection or leave the default name. Click "Finish" and then click OK. Click Ok again to close the wizard.

9. Right-click the second button and select "Button Properties". Click the "Rules" button. Click "Add" button. Click "Add Action" button. From the "Action", select "Close this form" and click OK. Click Ok thrice to close all the wizards.

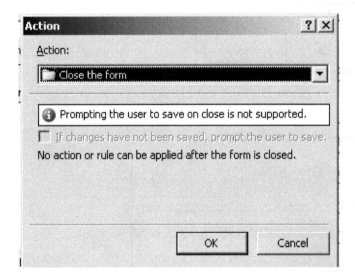

Figure 6.59: *Action*

10. Publish the form by selecting "Publish" from the "File" menu. Upgrade the form on the server. See previous article for help on this OR run the following commands from the command prompt:

```
stsadm.exe -o UpgradeFormTemplate -filename "C:\Forms\userregistrationtpl.xsn"

stsadm.exe -o execadmsvcjobs
```

Listing 6.22: *UpgradeFormTemplate*

Change file name and path in the "filename" parameter before running the commands.

Now, you have upgraded the form on the server. Open the form in the forms library and enter some dummy data and click the "Submit" button. The form will be submitted and you will see a javascript message.

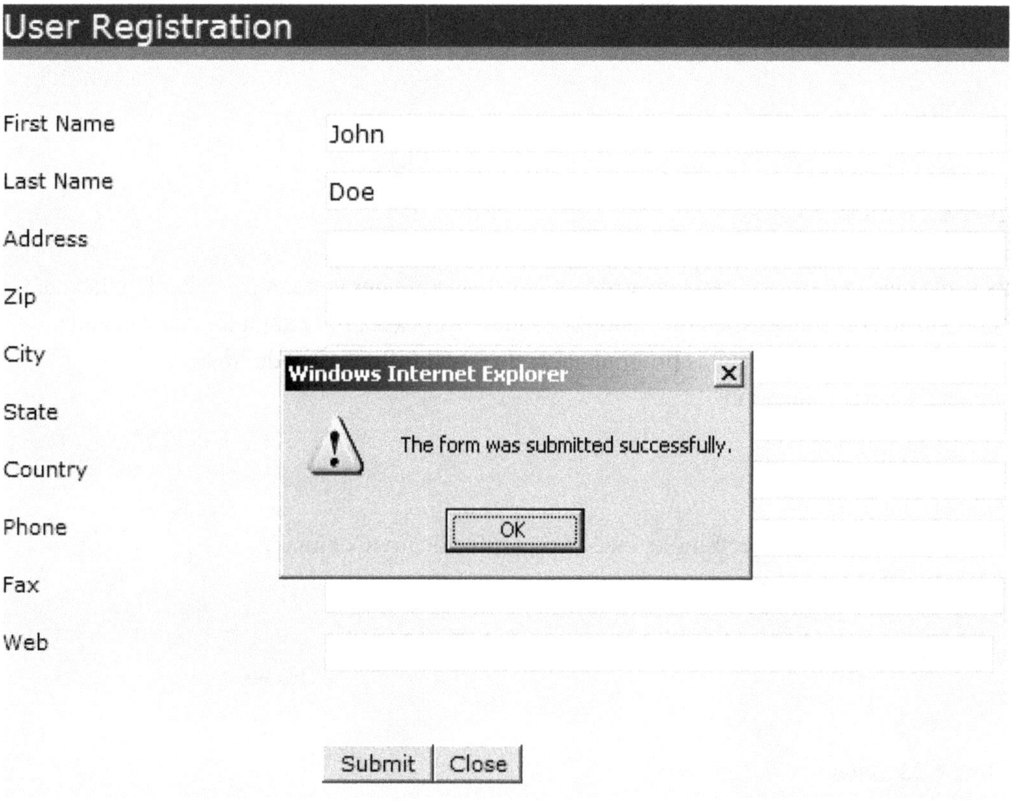

Figure 6.60: *Form submitted successfully*

Similarly, to test the close functionality, click the "Close" button. That will close the form.

Everything ok till now! Where is the fun part? The programming?

11. Right click the "Submit" button and select "Button Properties". From the "Action" drop down, select "Rules and Custom Code". This will change the label. Change the label back to "Submit". Now, click the "Edit Form Code" button. This will open the Visual studio. Visual Studio Tools for Applications (VSTA) must be installed on your machine for this to work.

12. You will see default code.

191

```
// NOTE: The following procedure is required by Microsoft Office InfoPath.
// It can be modified using Microsoft Office InfoPath.
public void InternalStartup()
{
    ((ButtonEvent)EventManager.ControlEvents["Submit"]).Clicked += new ClickedEventHe
}

public void Submit_Clicked(object sender, ClickedEventArgs e)
{
    // Write your code here.
}
}
```

Figure 6.61: *Submit_Clicked*

This is the place where you can play around. You can add your code in the Submit_Clicked() function to do something when the "Submit" button is clicked. For example, you can add a default value in one of the fields programmatically. Add following code in the "Submit_Clicked()" function:

```
XPathNavigator nav =
this.CreateNavigator().SelectSingleNode("/my:myFields/my:Country",
this.NamespaceManager);

nav.SetValue("USA");
```

Listing 6.23: *Submit_Clicked code*

This will set the value of "Country" field to "USA" when the "Submit" button is clicked. Let's add some more code. Add following code to the "Submit_Clicked()". This will submit the form programmatically.

```
FileSubmitConnection SubmitConnection =
(FileSubmitConnection)this.DataConnections["Main submit"];

SubmitConnection.FolderUrl = LibLocation.Substring(0, LibLocation.LastIndexOf("/"));

SubmitConnection.Execute();
```

Listing 6.24: *Execute connection*

Add FormEvents_Loading() function in the class.

```
public void FormEvents_Loading(object sender, LoadingEventArgs e)

{

}
```

Listing 6.25: *Form Loading event*

Add following code in FormEvents_Loading():

```
//Edit mode

if (e.InputParameters.ContainsKey("XmlLocation"))

{

Location = e.InputParameters["Source"].ToString();

Location = Location.Substring(0, Location.IndexOf("/", 8));

LibLocation = Location + e.InputParameters["XmlLocation"].ToString();

}
```

```
else

{

//New mode

LibLocation = e.InputParameters["SaveLocation"].ToString();

}
```

Listing 6.26: *Loading event code*

Add following event handler in "InternalStartup()" function:

```
EventManager.FormEvents.Loading += new LoadingEventHandler(FormEvents_Loading);
```

Listing 6.27: *InternalStartup()*

Finally, add the global variables to hold the form session data. These variables are used in the "Submit_Clicked()":

```
private string LibLocation
{
get
{
return (string)FormState["LibLocation"];
}
set
{
FormState["LibLocation"] = value;
}
}

private string Location
{
get
```

```
{
return (string)FormState["Location"];
}
set
{
FormState["Location"] = value;
}
}
```

Listing 6.28: *Global variables*

The complete code will look like this:

```
using Microsoft.Office.InfoPath;
using System;
using System.Xml;
using System.Xml.XPath;
namespace userregistration
{
public partial class FormCode
{
// Member variables are not supported in browser-enabled forms.
// Instead, write and read these values from the FormState
// dictionary using code such as the following:
//
// private object _memberVariable
// {
// get
// {
// return FormState["_memberVariable"];
// }
// set
// {
// FormState["_memberVariable"] = value;
// }
// }
// NOTE: The following procedure is required by Microsoft Office InfoPath.
// It can be modified using Microsoft Office InfoPath.
```

```
public void InternalStartup()
{
EventManager.FormEvents.Loading += new LoadingEventHandler(FormEvents_Loading);
((ButtonEvent)EventManager.ControlEvents["Submit"]).Clicked += new
ClickedEventHandler(Submit_Clicked);
}
private string LibLocation
{
get
{
return (string)FormState["LibLocation"];
}
set
{
FormState["LibLocation"] = value;
}
}
private string Location
{
get
{
return (string)FormState["Location"];
}
set
{
FormState["Location"] = value;
}
}
public void FormEvents_Loading(object sender, LoadingEventArgs e)
{
//Edit mode
if (e.InputParameters.ContainsKey("XmlLocation"))
{
Location = e.InputParameters["Source"].ToString();
Location = Location.Substring(0, Location.IndexOf("/", 8));
LibLocation = Location + e.InputParameters["XmlLocation"].ToString();
}
else
{
//New mode
```

```
LibLocation = e.InputParameters["SaveLocation"].ToString();
}
}
public void Submit_Clicked(object sender, ClickedEventArgs e)
{
XPathNavigator nav =
this.CreateNavigator().SelectSingleNode("/my:myFields/my:Country",
this.NamespaceManager);
nav.SetValue("USA");
FileSubmitConnection SubmitConnection =
(FileSubmitConnection)this.DataConnections["Main submit"];
SubmitConnection.FolderUrl = LibLocation.Substring(0, LibLocation.LastIndexOf("/"));
SubmitConnection.Execute();
}
}
}
```

Listing 6.29: *Complete code*

13. Compile the code (Build > Build <form name>). Re-publish the form. Go to forms library and open the form. Add First and Last name. Click the "Submit" button. You will notice the "Country" field will be populated with "USA". The form has been saved in the library. Close the form and you will see a link in the library.

Download application:

http://walisystems.com/articles/SPS/programming/userregistration.zip

Populating InfoPath Drop down with SharePoint List Data

In this section, I will show you how to populate a drop down in InfoPath form with data retrieved from a SharePoint list.

We will continue using the user registration form that we created in one of the previous sections. The country field, which we added as a text box, will be converted to a drop down box.

1. We will need a list on the SharePoint that will hold all country names. Create a list in SharePoint and add some countries. Name the list "Countries". Use "Title" field to store the country names.

Figure 6.62: *SharePoint List*

2. Open the user registration form in InfoPath editor.

3. Right-click the "Country" text box and move your mouse to "Change To" option, that will open another menu. Select "Drop-Down List Box". This will convert the text box into a drop down box.

198

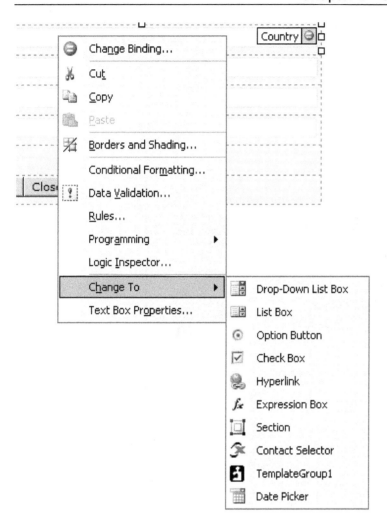

Figure 6.63: *Change text box to drop down box*

4. Right-click the drop down and select "Drop-Down List Box Properties"

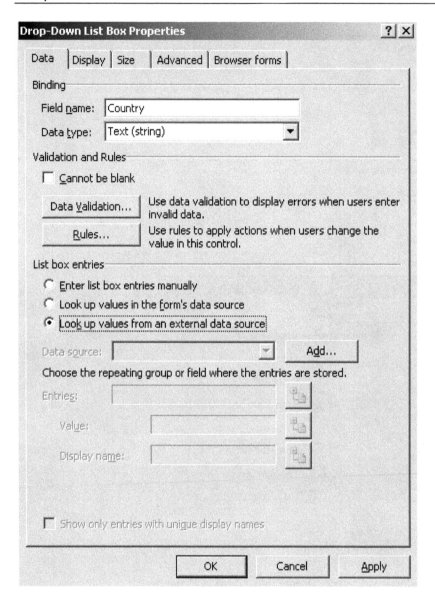

Figure 6.64: *Drop down list box properties*

5. In "List box entries", select the third option "Look up values from an external data source".

6. Click the "Add" button.

7. In the "Data Connection Wizard", select "Create a new connection to:". Sub-option "Receive data" will automatically be selected. "Submit data" will be disabled, this is because you cannot submit data to a drop down. Click "Next:.

200

Figure 6.65: *Data connection wizard*

8. Select "SharePoint library or list" from the options and click "Next:.

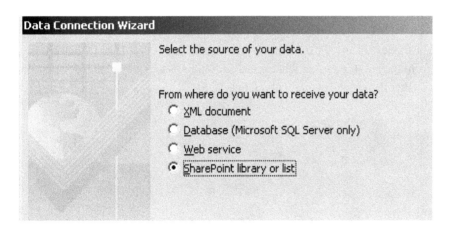

Figure 6.66: *Data connection wizard – Receive data*

9. Enter the SharePoint site collection URL and click "Next".

10. You will be shown all the lists on the server. Select "Countries" list and click "Next"

11. You will see a list of fields. We saved country names in "Title" field, so select "Title" field and click "Next".

12. Check "Store a copy of the data in the form template" option and click "Next".

13.You can change the name of data connection in this step. The default name is "Countries" which is the list name. Make sure the checkbox "Automatically retrieve data when form is opened" is checked and click "Finish".

14. You will be back in the "Drop-Down List Box Properties". Click the "Select XPath" button.

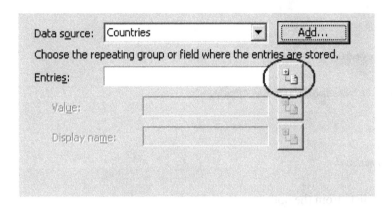

Figure 6.67: *Selecting drop down source*

15. Expand "dataFields" node. Select ":Title" node. You will also see "Filter Data..." button. It filters data retrieved from the list. It's a great feature but does not work in web enabled forms. In web forms, we have to filter data programmatically. Click "OK".

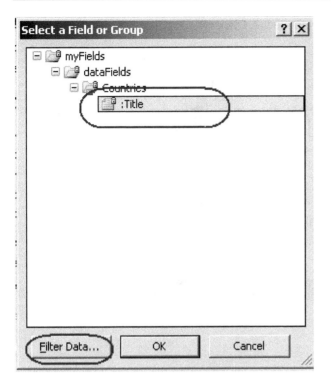

Figure 6.68: *Filter data*

16. Had there been multiple columns in the list, we could have selected a value different from the display name. Yes, you can select different list columns to be used as drop down value and drop down display name. Because we are only using one field, therefore, only "Title" field is selected in both "Value" and "Display name" fields.

Figure 6.69: *Drop down properties*

17. Check "Show only entries with unique display names" option. This is in fact not required here because we know the names will be unique but if the list has duplicate names, then this

option allows us to select unique names from the list. Click OK.

Show only entries with unique display names
OK
Cancel
Apply

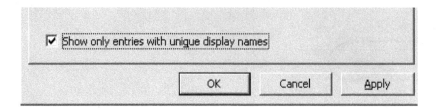

Figure 6.70: *Show only unique items*

18. Publish the form and test the functionality. Open the form, the "Country" drop down will show all countries form the list.

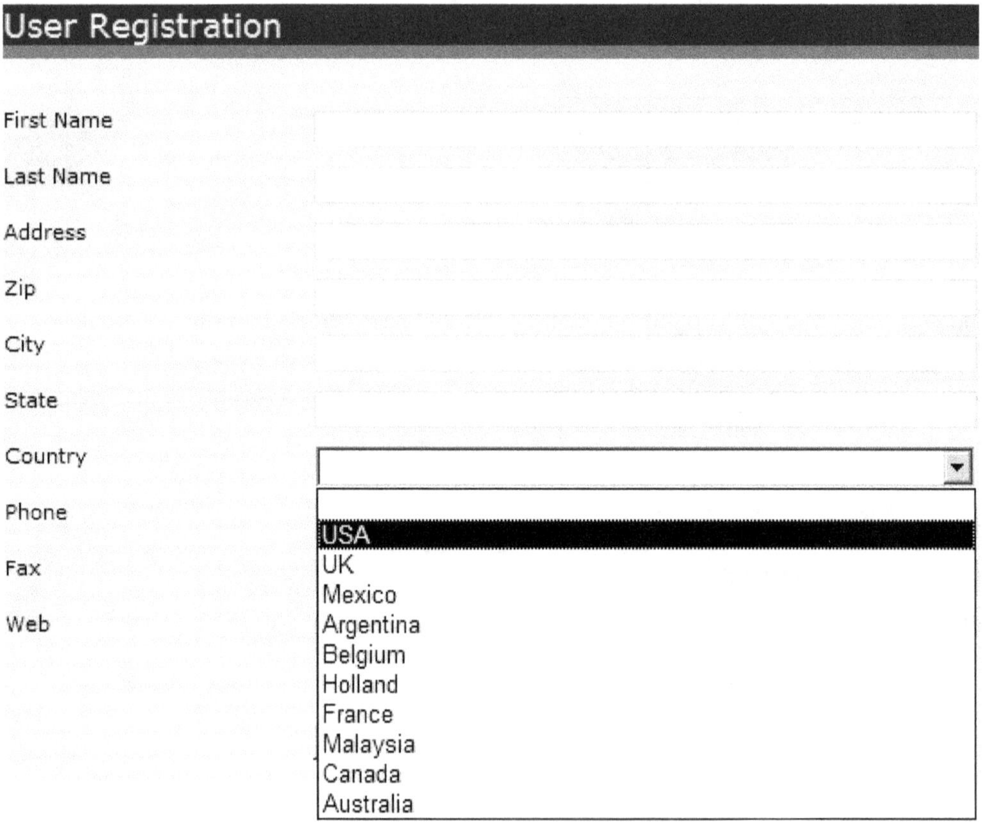

User Registration
First Name
Last Name
Address
Zip
City
State
Country
Phone
Fax
Web
USA
UK
Mexico
Argentina
Belgium
Holland
France
Malaysia
Canada
Australia

Figure 6.71: *User Registration Form*

There is a draw back to this method. If you deploy this form on a different server. The functionality will break because the data connection will still be pointing to the list on the development machine. There are other methods to achieve correct behavior. One of them is to do it programmatically. We will discuss it next.

Download completed InfoPath form and application code:

http://walisystems.com/articles/SPS/dropdown/dropdown.zip

Retrieving data from a SharePoint list

There can be different scenarios in InfoPath where programming can be needed. Professional applications cannot be complete without some sort of programming effort. InfoPath is designed in a way that makes creating forms very easy for the users. You can create complicated forms without coding anything but large organizations try to leverage full benefits of InfoPath and full benefits can only be had by adding value to the forms by using complex programming techniques. In this article, we are going to use a simple programming technique that will show you how to populate a drop down box in InfoPath form programmatically with data from a SharePoint list. Of course, there is a way to do it without programming, for example, you can use a data connection to populate the drop down but suppose you want to populate the drop down in a particular scenario or in other words, we can say that you want to populate it dynamically depending on business logic in the form. There can be literally hundreds of scenarios. The biggest advantage of using programming to achieve this goal is you don't have to worry that your data connection will break after deploying to the form to some other server which is a very common problem.

1. Open "user registration" form in InfoPath editor.

2. Add a new data source. Right-click "myFields" in data sources and click "Add".

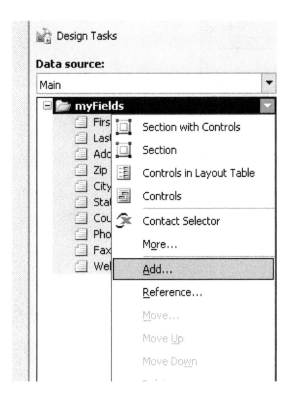

Figure 6.72: *Design Tasks*

3. Add "Countries" as a name. From "Type", select "Group" and check "Repeating" checkbox at the bottom and click OK. This will add a repeating group in the data sources.

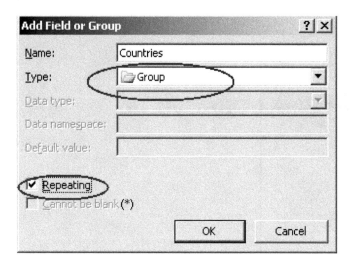

Figure 6.73: *Add field or group*

4. Right-click the newly added group "Countries" and select "Add".

5. We will add two fields (elements). Add "Displayname" in the "Name" box. Leave all other options as they are.

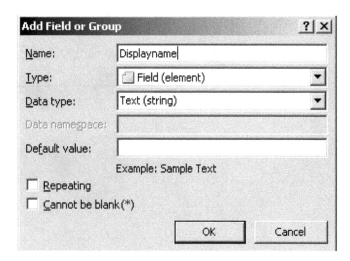

Figure 6.74: *Field Displayname*

6. Repeat steps 4 and 5 to add another field and name it "Value".

7. Right-click the "Country" drop down in the form and select "Drop-Down List Box

Properties".

8. Select "Look up values in the form's data source" option in the "List box entries".

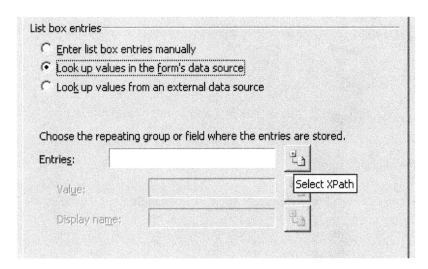

Figure 6.75: *Look up values in the form's data source*

9. Click "Select XPath" button.

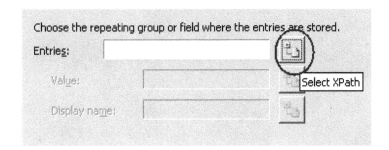

Figure 6.76: *Select XPath*

10. Select "Countries" (repeating group) and click OK.

11. "Value" and "Display name" will automatically be populated. Change the value in "Value" box by clicking the "Select XPath" button and selecting "Value". Click OK to close the properties.

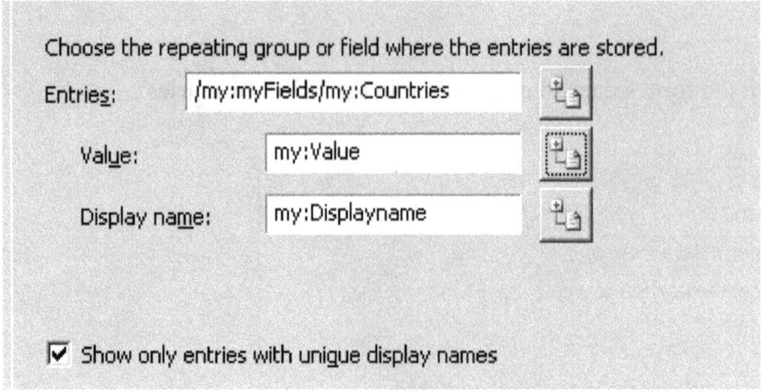

Choose the repeating group or field where the entries are stored.

Entries: /my:myFields/my:Countries

Value: my:Value

Display name: my:Displayname

☑ Show only entries with unique display names

Figure 6.77: *Show unique items*

12. Open VSTA by selecting Tools > Programming > Microsoft Visual Studio Tools For Applications.

13. Add a reference to "Microsoft.SharePoint.DLL".

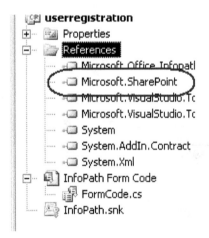

Figure 6.78: *Add reference*

The DLL is located in the following folder:

System Drive:\Program Files\Common Files\Microsoft Shared\web server extensions\12\ISAPI

14. Add a reference in code.

```
using Microsoft.SharePoint;
```

Listing 6.30: *Add reference*

15. In the FormEvents_Loading(),. add following function:

```
//Populate country drop down

AddCountries();
```

Listing 6.31: *Call AddCountries function*

16. The code for AddCountries() is as following:

```
public void AddCountries()

{

try

{

SPSite site = SPContext.Current.Site;

SPWeb web = site.OpenWeb();

SPList list = web.Lists["Countries"];

SPListItemCollection listitems = list.Items;

XPathNavigator nav =
this.CreateNavigator().SelectSingleNode("/my:myFields/my:Countries",
this.NamespaceManager);
```

```
foreach (SPListItem li in listitems)

{

XPathNavigator newNode = null;

newNode = nav.Clone();

newNode.SelectSingleNode("/my:myFields/my:Countries/my:Displayname",
this.NamespaceManager).SetValue(li["Title"].ToString());

newNode.SelectSingleNode("/my:myFields/my:Countries /my:Value",
this.NamespaceManager).SetValue(li["Title"].ToString());

nav.InsertAfter(newNode);

newNode = null;

}

nav.DeleteSelf();

nav = null;

}

catch

{

}

}
```

Listing 6.32: *Function AddCountries*

17. Compile the project, publish the form and open it in SharePoint, here is what you should see:

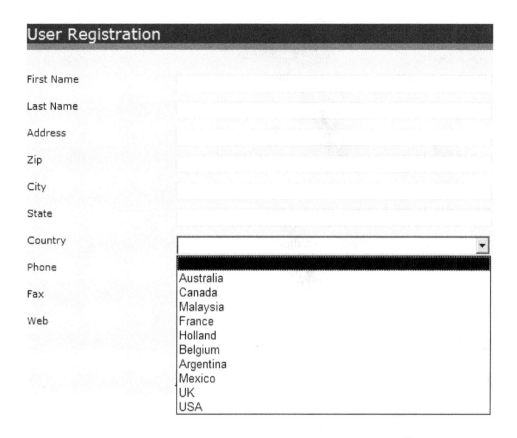

Figure 6.79: *User registration form*

18. This is the programmatic solution. You don't have to worry that your data connection will break on another server. Let's discuss the code briefly. This is not an efficient method of populating the drop down. We should have used SPQuery() object to get data from the list. SPQuery is fast and efficient and works very well with large lists but here our objective was not to achieve efficiency but to show how to fetch data programmatically. We get site context using the "SPContext". You can also hard code the site URL but that's not a good idea. We cannot hard code paths in professional applications. After creating the listitem collection, we read each list item from the collection in a loop. Before getting into the loop, we create a main node that points to the "Countries" repeating group. In the for loop, we create a clone of this node and add values to the "Value" and "Displayname" elements. "Value" and "Displayname" fields get their values from the list item.

213

```
newNode.SelectSingleNode("/my:myFields/my:Countries/my:Displayname",
this.NamespaceManager).SetValue(li["Title"].ToString());

newNode.SelectSingleNode("/my:myFields/my:Countries/my:Value",
this.NamespaceManager).SetValue(li["Title"].ToString());
```

Listing 6.33: *Setting node values*

After you set the values, you have to insert this cloned node in the nodes hierarchy. You do this using the "InsertAfter() method:

```
nav.InsertAfter(newNode);
```

Listing 6.34: *Add event handler*

"newNode" is passed as a parameter to the "InsertAfter()" method.

After you leave the for loop, you must destroy the parent node that was used to create cloned nodes. This is important to avoid duplicate entry of the parent node otherwise you will see first entry as duplicates.

```
nav.DeleteSelf();
```

Listing 6.35: *Delete node*

You can download the form and complete application from the following link:

http://walisystems.com/articles/SPS/dropdown2/sharepoint_list_data.zip

Retrieving data from a SharePoint list using SPQuery

Drop Down Box Items Sorting

In previous section, you saw how to retrieve data from a SharePoint list programmatically. In this section, you will modify code and make it more efficient by using the SPQuery object. SPQuery will make the code efficient and fast. It will also sort the items and the drop down will show a sorted list of countries.

1. Open form (http://walisystems.com/articles/SPS/dropdown2/userregistrationtpl.xsn) in editor. (Note: Download the form to your hard disk first and then open it in editor)

2. Open VSTA.

3. Modify the AddCountries() function by adding these lines:

```
SPQuery query = new SPQuery();

query.Query = "<OrderBy><FieldRef Name='Title' /></OrderBy>";
```

Listing 6.36: *Define SPQuery object*

Then modify the statement in the same function that defined list item collection:

```
SPListItemCollection listitems = list.Items;
```

Listing 6.37: *Old definition of listitems*

215

The new statement will be:

```
SPListItemCollection listitems = list.GetItems(query);
```

Listing 6.38: *New definition of listitems*

You will notice the query is missing the "<Where>" tag. This is because we are not filtering the data. "<Where>" tag is used to filter data. Right now we are just sorting the data. To sort data, we use "<OrderBy>" tag. The complete code will look like the following:

```
public void AddCountries()

{

try

{

SPSite site = SPContext.Current.Site;

SPWeb web = site.OpenWeb();

SPList list = web.Lists["Countries"];

SPQuery query = new SPQuery();

query.Query = "<OrderBy><FieldRef Name='Title' /></OrderBy>";

SPListItemCollection listitems = list.GetItems(query);

XPathNavigator nav =
this.CreateNavigator().SelectSingleNode("/my:myFields/my:Countries",
this.NamespaceManager);

foreach (SPListItem li in listitems)
```

```
{

XPathNavigator newNode = null;

newNode = nav.Clone();

newNode.SelectSingleNode("/my:myFields/my:Countries/my:Displayname",
this.NamespaceManager).SetValue(li["Title"].ToString());

newNode.SelectSingleNode("/my:myFields/my:Countries /my:Value",
this.NamespaceManager).SetValue(li["Title"].ToString());

nav.InsertAfter(newNode);

newNode = null;

}

nav.DeleteSelf();

nav = null;

}

catch

{

}

}
```

Listing 6.39: *Function AddCountries()*

4. You don't have to make any changes in your form. Compile the code, republish the form, open it in SharePoint and you will see a sorted list of countries in the "Country" drop down.

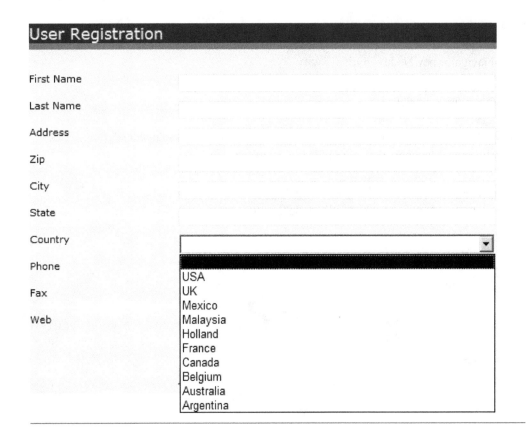

Figure 6.80: *User Registration form*

You will notice that the list has been sorted in the reverse order. To sort it in correct order, change the query. Add attribute "Ascending='FALSE'" in the query.

```
query.Query = "<OrderBy><FieldRef Name='Title' Ascending='FALSE' /></OrderBy>";
```

Listing 6.40: *SPQuery*

Now, the list will be sorted with countries starting with alphabet "A" first.

Download completed InfoPath form and application code (ZIP format):

http://walisystems.com/articles/SPS/dropdown3/dropdown3.zip

Showing filtered items in InfoPath drop down

Drop Down Box Items Filtering

We have seen sorting of items, now we will see how to filter the items in a drop down. Remember, the built-in filtering feature of the drop down does not work in web enabled forms.

1. Open "user registration" form (http://walisystems.com/articles/SPS/dropdown3/userregistrationtpl.xsn) in Editor. (Note: Download the form to your hard disk first and then open in editor)

2. Open VSTA.

3. Modify the code. Now that you know how to use the SPQuery object, you just need to change the query to get the desired results. Filtering can be done on any column of the list but just to demo you the process, I will keep it simple. We will apply the filter on the "title" field. The query will return countries that start with alphabet "U". This is simple. You can add more filters as and when you like. Add the following to the query definition:

```
<Where><BeginsWith><FieldRef Name='Title' /><Value
Type='Text'>U</Value></BeginsWith></Where>
```

Listing 6.41: Query definition

"<BeginsWith>" tag is used to search the start of columns that hold Text or Node field type values. We pass "U" so the query will search for the items that start with "U".

Here is the complete function:

```
public void AddCountries()

{

try
```

```
{

SPSite site = SPContext.Current.Site;

SPWeb web = site.OpenWeb();

SPList list = web.Lists["Countries"];

SPQuery query = new SPQuery();

query.Query = "<Where><BeginsWith><FieldRef Name='Title' /><Value
Type='Text'>U</Value></BeginsWith></Where>"

+ "<OrderBy><FieldRef Name='Title' Ascending='FALSE' /></OrderBy>";

SPListItemCollection listitems = list.GetItems(query);

XPathNavigator nav =
this.CreateNavigator().SelectSingleNode("/my:myFields/my:Countries",
this.NamespaceManager);

foreach (SPListItem li in listitems)

{

XPathNavigator newNode = null;

newNode = nav.Clone();

newNode.SelectSingleNode("/my:myFields/my:Countries/my:Displayname",
this.NamespaceManager).SetValue(li["Title"].ToString());

newNode.SelectSingleNode("/my:myFields/my:Countries /my:Value",
this.NamespaceManager).SetValue(li["Title"].ToString());

nav.InsertAfter(newNode);

newNode = null;
```

```
}

nav.DeleteSelf();

nav = null;

}

catch

{

}

}
```

Listing 6.42: *Function AddCountries()*

Here is how the drop down will look like:

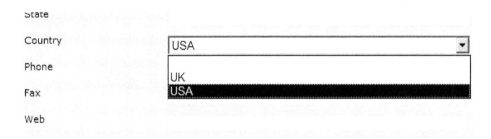

Figure 6.81: *Filtered drop down*

Drop down only shows countries that start with a "U".

Download completed InfoPath form and application code (ZIP format):

http://walisystems.com/articles/SPS/dropdown4/dropdown4.zip

Summary

This chapter primarily focused on the development side. InfoPath is a popular product that is used to create electronic forms. InfoPath is commonly used with SharePoint. Companies publish electronic forms created with InfoPath on SharePoint. They basically use SharePoint as a distribution channel for the electronic forms. With the advent of browser-enabled electronic forms in InfoPath 2007, InfoPath became more popular than ever and formed an excellent combination with SharePoint to provide companies a development platform. Both InfoPath and SharePoint go hand in hand when it comes to the development and sharing of electronic forms. The first topic in this chapter focused on checking the design of the InfoPath form. Forms, if not developed using the best practices, can be slow and will give sloppy performance. InfoPath provides a built-in tool to check the design of the form. This chapter gives practical solutions that users can use as hands-on exercises to learn development with InfoPath and SharePoint. An important topic discussed in this chapter is the publishing of the forms. That is the most important section. Forms, after they have been developed, have to be published in InfoPath. InfoPath provides a way to publish the form using the built-in wizard but the browser-enabled forms have to be published on your hard disk first and then uploaded to the SharePoint as administrator approved forms. Stsadm.exe is a fantastic tool that has many uses. One of the uses is to deploy InfoPath forms. You learned the usage of this tool by seeing practical examples. You saw practical examples on how to write code for reading and writing data to SharePoint lists.

Chapter 7

Development with SharePoint

In this chapter:

- Creating a custom web service for SharePoint
- Consuming web service in SharePoint
- Technoservice: a programming sample
- Deploying web service using SharePoint designer
- Installing a web service
- Creating an installer for your custom developed web service
- Technopart: a web part programming sample
- WS-Downloader: an application that downloads documents from SharePoint
- WS-Downloader web part: web part that downloads documents from SharePoint
- MOSS 2007 Upload Tool: Download an upload tool to see and learn programming by example
- Creating list definition and WSP for a SharePoint list
- Creating SharePoint list view dynamically

I gave some programming tips and examples in Chapter 6 "InfoPath and SharePoint". In this chapter, we will explore some more techniques. I will give you some programming examples. This chapter also covers some tools (web services, web parts, etc) that you can download and experiment with to hone your SharePoint programming skills.

Creating a Custom Web Service for SharePoint

Category: Microsoft Office SharePoint Server 2007, Windows SharePoint Services 3.0

There are a couple of Microsoft articles available on the internet that walk you through the creation process. Here are the links:

Walkthrough: Creating a Custom Web Service (Windows SharePoint Services 3.0)
(http://msdn2.microsoft.com/en-us/library/ms464040.aspx)

Writing Custom Web Services for SharePoint Products and Technologies (SharePoint Portal Server 2003)
(http://msdn2.microsoft.com/en-gb/library/ms916810.aspx)

If you are an experienced SharePoint developer, then the articles mentioned above should be enough to get you started but if you are a developer who is new to SharePoint development and you are looking to create your first web service for SharePoint then go ahead, read this article. This article will guide you through the process of creating a custom web service for SharePoint. This web service will work with new versions of SharePoint, Office SharePoint Server 2007 and Windows SharePoint Service 3.0. We will create a simple service that will upload documents to SharePoint. We will call it UploadService. Remember, there are steps in the Microsoft articles that are confusing especially for the beginners, I have taken care of that as well. I have tried to include as much information as possible including screenshots and code snippets to make the job easier for the developer.

Basic Steps for Creating a Web Service

- Create an ASP.NET web service in Microsoft Visual Studio 2005. There are two ways to do this. You can develop a web service on the server machine that hosts SharePoint or you can develop it on a remote machine that does not host SharePoint and later deploy the service on the machine that hosts SharePoint. We will discuss the second method in this article.
- Add .ASMX file to your project if it's not already there. This file will contain the programming logic for the web service. Note, you can add programming logic to the markup page as well as the code behind. The choice is yours.
- Generate a static discovery file (disco) and a Web Services Description Language (WSDL) file.
- Modify the disco and wsdl files for SharePoint.
- Deploy the web service files to the SharePoint server.
- Create a client application to consume the web service.

About the Sample Application

You can download the sample application (web service) from the following link:

http://www.walisystems.com/ws1_dlc.asp

Download size is 361 KB.

The zip file contains the web service and its related files. It also contains an installer to help you install the service easily on your server. Unzip the file to your hard disk. It will create a "WSUploadService" folder. You can unzip the file anywhere on your hard disk. There is no restriction on unzipping it to a particular folder. Run "UploadServiceCopier.exe" to install the service. Installer will ask you to select a SharePoint site where this service should be installed. Select your site from the drop down and keep the folder name as "bin" (second field: textbox) and click "Next".

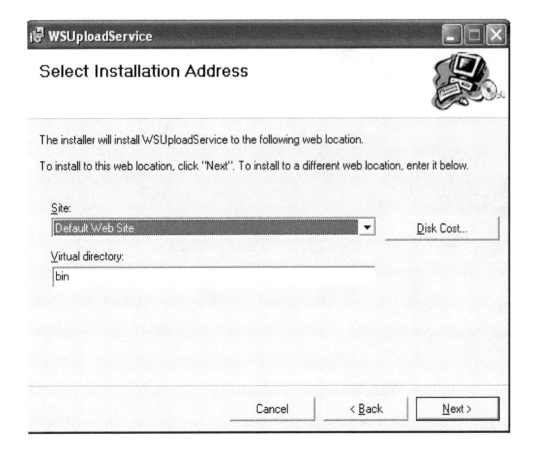

Figure 7.1: *Select Installation Address*

To uninstall, run the "UploadServiceCopier.exe" again. It will give you the following message:

"Service is already installed. Do you want to uninstall it?"

Select "Yes" and then select "Remove WSUploadService" and click "Finish" to uninstall the service. Uninstall will remove all copied files from your hard disk.

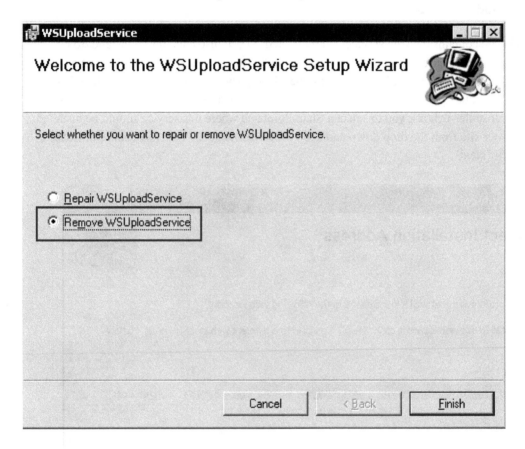

Figure 7.2: *Uninstall*

Please run "UploadServiceCopier.exe" to install/uninstall the service. Do not run "setup.exe" directly as it will not install the service correctly.

Creating a Custom Web Service

1. The first step is to create an ASP.NET web service project in Visual Studio 2005. If you don't find a web service project template in visual studio, that means that you are still running an old

version of Visual Studio 2005, the one without the service pack. You will have to download and install the Visual Studio 2005 Service Pack 1 Beta from the Microsoft. Here is the link:

http://www.microsoft.com/downloads/details.aspx?familyid=8D702463-674B-4978-9E22-C989130F6553&displaylang=en

It's a 371.9 MB download and let me tell you in advance that the installation is very slow and takes a lot of time.

On the **File** menu, click **New Project**.

2. In the **Project Types** box, select **Visual C#.**

3. In the **Templates** box, select **ASP.NET Web Service Application**.

4. In the **Name** box, type **UploadService**. In the Location box, type the following path:

C:\WebService

You can also click the **browse** button to browse the folders and select the destination folder. This is the path where the project will be stored.

In the **Solution Name** box, type **UploadService** and check **Create directory for solution** checkbox.

5. Click **OK**.

6. In the Solution Explorer, right-click **Service1.asmx** and rename the file **Files.asmx** and then right click **Files.asmx** and click **View Code**.

7. Add a reference to the assembly for Microsoft Office SharePoint Server 2007 (**Microsoft.SharePoint.dll**). This assembly is located in the following directory:

C:\Program Files\Common Files\Microsoft Shared\web server extensions\12\ISAPI

Please note that if you are developing on a machine that does not have SharePoint installed then you can copy the required files from the SharePoint machine to your development machine.

8. Make sure following **using** directives are included at the top:

```
using Microsoft.SharePoint;
using Microsoft.SharePoint.WebControls;
using System.Net;
```

Listing 7.1: *Including classes*

9. Change your class name from Service1 to **Files**.

```
public class Files : System.Web.Services.WebService
```

Listing 7.2: *Change File name*

10. Comment out the web method definition. The commented out web method code will look like as follows:

```
//[WebMethod]
//public string HelloWorld()
//{
//return "Hello World";
//}
```

Listing 7.3: *Web Method*

11. Add following code (web method) in the class:

```
[WebMethod]
public string UploadDocument(string fileName, byte[] fileContents, string pathFolder)
{
  if (fileContents == null)
  {
    return "Null Attachment";
  }

  try
  {
    int iStartIndex = pathFolder.LastIndexOf("/");
    string sitePath = pathFolder.Remove(iStartIndex);
    string folderName = pathFolder.Substring(iStartIndex + 1);

    SPSite site = new SPSite(sitePath);
    SPWeb web = site.OpenWeb();

    SPFolder folder = web.GetFolder(folderName);

    string fileURL = fileName;

    folder.Files.Add(fileURL, fileContents);

    if (folder.Files[fileURL].CheckedOutBy.Name != "")
    {
      folder.Files[fileURL].CheckIn("File Checked In");
    }

    return "File added successfully!";

  }
  catch (System.Exception ex)
  {
    return "Error: " + ex.Source + " - " + ex.Message;
  }
}
```

Listing 7.4: *Web Method code*

12. Open **Files.asmx** markup page. In **Solution Explorer**, right-click **Files.asmx** and select **View Markup**. You will notice that the markup page has following line:

```
<%@ WebService Language="C#" CodeBehind="Service1.asmx.cs"
Class="UploadService.Service1" %>
```

Listing 7.5: *Definition*

Change it to the following line:

```
<%@ WebService Language="C#" Class="UploadService.Files" %>
```

Listing 7.6: *Modified Definition*

13. Create a strong name for the class library. In **Solution Explorer**, right-click the web service project, and in the **Properties** dialog box, click **Signing**, select **Sign the assembly**, and select **<New>** in the box for choosing a strong name key file.

14. In the **Create Strong Name Key** dialog box, provide a file name for the key, deselect **Protect my key file with a password**, and click **OK**.

TIP

This was the easy way. You can also strong name your assembly using the command line utility called as sn.exe. Use following steps if you want to strong name your assembly manually:

1. Strong naming utility (sn.exe) can be found in the following folder:

C:\Program Files\Microsoft Visual Studio 8\SDK\v2.0\Bin

Copy the sn.exe utility to the folder where your assembly is located and run the following command to strong name your assembly:

---

sn.exe -k key.snk

Resulting key will be written to the key.snk file.

2. Go to your project's properties (right-click project name in the **Solution Explorer** and select **Properties** from the menu) and select **Signing** from the menu that appears on the left. This will open a form.

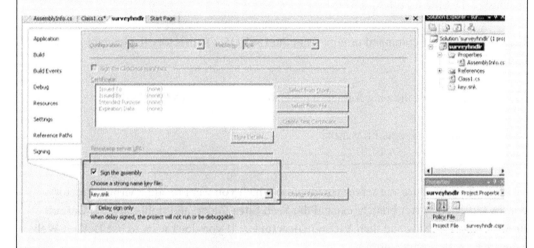

Figure 7.3: *Sign the assembly*

3. Check **Sign the assembly** checkbox and choose the key file from the drop down (Click the **Browse...** button in the drop down to locate the key.snk file that you generated in the previous step).

4. Re-compile your assembly.

15. Compile the web service project.

16. As we are developing this web service on a machine that does not host SharePoint, therefore, we need to create a virtual directory in IIS. Click **Start**, point to **Administrative Tools** (You may have to go to the **Control Panel** first to select **Administrative Tools**), and then click **Internet Information Services (IIS) Manager**.

Note: In case you are developing the service on a SharePoint server, then skip steps 17-20 and use following instructions and then start with step 22:

1. Copy the Files.asmx to the following folder:

C:\Program Files\Common Files\Microsoft Shared\web server extensions\12\TEMPLATE\LAYOUTS

2. Run disco.exe at the command prompt from the **LAYOUTS** directory to generate .disco and .wsdl files.

Run a command in the following format to generate the files in **LAYOUTS**:

disco http://localhost/_layouts/Files.asmx

17. Expand the branch for the server computer to which you want to add a virtual directory. Under the server computer branch, expand the **Web Sites** folder, and right-click the **Default Web Site** and select **New** and then **Virtual Directory...**. If you don't want to use Default Web Site, you can create a new web site.

18. Click **Next** and enter an alias in the text box, for example, for this service you can enter **UploadService**.

19. Click **Next** and then click **Browse...** button to browse to the project folder (containing the .asmx file) and click **Next**.

20. Click **Next** again and then click **Finish**.

Generating and Modifying Static Discovery and WSDL Files

21. Use Disco.exe to generate .disco and .wsdl files. This command line utility is located in the following directory:

C:\Program Files\Microsoft Visual Studio 8\SDK\v2.0\Bin

Open command prompt and type the following line and press Enter:

Disco http://localhost/uploadservice/Files.asmx

Make sure you have entered the correct path in the command above otherwise you will get an error. If you created a virtual directory on a port other than the port 80, then you must mention the port number in the path (For example, http://localhost:8080/uploadservice/Files.asmx). This will generate the .disco and .wsdl files.

22. To register namespaces of the Windows SharePoint Services object model, open both the .disco and .wsdl files and replace the opening XML processing instruction -- <?xml version="1.0" encoding="utf-8"?> -- with instructions such as the following:

```
<%@ Page Language="C#" Inherits="System.Web.UI.Page"%> <%@ Assembly
Name="Microsoft.SharePoint, Version=12.0.0.0, Culture=neutral,
PublicKeyToken=71e9bce111e9429c" %> <%@ Import
Namespace="Microsoft.SharePoint.Utilities" %> <%@ Import
Namespace="Microsoft.SharePoint" %> <% Response.ContentType = "text/xml"; %>
```

Listing 7.7: *Register namespaces*

23. In the .disco file, modify the contract reference and SOAP address tags to be like the following example, which replaces literal paths with code generated paths through use of the Microsoft.SharePoint.Utilities.SPEncode class, and which replaces the method name that is specified in the **binding** attribute:

```
<contractRef ref=<%
SPHttpUtility.AddQuote(SPHttpUtility.HtmlEncode(SPWeb.OriginalBaseUrl(Request) +
"?wsdl"),Response.Output=""); %> docRef=<%
SPHttpUtility.AddQuote(SPHttpUtility.HtmlEncode(SPWeb.OriginalBaseUrl(Request)),Re
sponse.Output); %> xmlns="http://schemas.xmlsoap.org/disco/scl/" /> <soap address=<%
SPHttpUtility.AddQuote(SPHttpUtility.HtmlEncode(SPWeb.OriginalBaseUrl(Request)),Re
sponse.Output); %> xmlns:q1="http://tempuri.org" binding="q1:FilesSoap"
xmlns="http://schemas.xmlsoap.org/disco/soap/" /> <soap address=<%
SPHttpUtility.AddQuote(SPHttpUtility.HtmlEncode(SPWeb.OriginalBaseUrl(Request)),Re
sponse.Output); %> xmlns:q2="http://tempuri.org" binding="q2:FilesSoap12"
xmlns="http://schemas.xmlsoap.org/disco/soap/" />
```

Listing 7.8: *Modify .disco file*

233

24. In the .wsdl file, make the following, similar substitution for the SOAP address that is specified:

```
<soap:address location=<%
SPHttpUtility.AddQuote(SPHttpUtility.HtmlEncode(SPWeb.OriginalBaseUrl(Request)),Re
sponse.Output); %> />
```

Listing 7.9: *soap tag*

Make the following substitution for the SOAP12 address:

```
<soap12:address location=<%
SPHttpUtility.AddQuote(SPHttpUtility.HtmlEncode(SPWeb.OriginalBaseUrl(Request)),Re
sponse.Output); %> />
```

Listing 7.10: *Modify soap tag*

25. Rename both files in the respective formats Filedisco.aspx and Fileswsdl.aspx so that your service is discoverable through SharePoint.

Deploying web service on the SharePoint server

Copy the Web service files to the _vti_bin virtual directory

26. Copy the web service files to the **_vti_bin** directory of the SharePoint server. Web service files that are to be copied are as following:

Files.asmx
Filesdisco.aspx
Fileswsdl.aspx

The **_vti_bin** virtual directory maps physically to the *Local_Drive*:\Program Files\Common Files\Microsoft Shared\Web Server Extensions\12\ISAPI directory, which contains the default Web service files used in Windows SharePoint Services.

To include the Web service in the list of web services on the server

27. In Notepad, open the spsdisco.aspx file. spsdisco.aspx is located in the following directory (on the SharePoint server):

Local_Drive:\Program Files\Common Files\Microsoft Shared\web server extensions\12\ISAPI

28. Add the following lines to the end of the file within the **discovery** element and save the file:

```
<contractRef ref=<% SPHttpUtility.AddQuote(SPHttpUtility.HtmlEncode(spWeb.Url +
"/_vti_bin/Files.asmx?wsdl"), Response.Output); %> docRef=<%
SPHttpUtility.AddQuote(SPHttpUtility.HtmlEncode(spWeb.Url + "/_vti_bin/Files.asmx"),
Response.Output); %> xmlns="http://schemas.xmlsoap.org/disco/scl/" />
<soap address=<% SPHttpUtility.AddQuote(SPHttpUtility.HtmlEncode(spWeb.Url +
"/_vti_bin/Files.asmx"), Response.Output); %>
xmlns:q1="http://schemas.microsoft.com/sharepoint/soap/directory/"
binding="q1:FilesSoap" xmlns="http://schemas.xmlsoap.org/disco/soap/" />
```

Listing 7.11: *Modify discovery element*

Copying the assembly to the correct Bin folder

29. I have seen blogs and forums where people have recommended to copy the assembly to the following folder:

Local_Drive:\program files\common files\microsoft shared\web server extensions\12\isapi\

Some people say it should be copied to the following folder:

Local_Drive:\Inetpub\wwwroot\bin

bin folder is not there by default and has to be created but safest place to copy the assembly is the **bin** folder of the virtual directory of the web application where you intend to use the web service. Following path contains the virtual directories of web applications that you have created on your SharePoint server.

Local_Drive:\Inetpub\wwwroot\wss\VirtualDirectories

For example, if you want to use the web service in web application at port 81, then you should copy the assembly to the following folder:

Local_Drive:\Inetpub\wwwroot\wss\VirtualDirectories\81\bin

Similarly, if you want to use the web service in web application at port 17316, then you should copy the assembly to the following folder:

Local_Drive:\Inetpub\wwwroot\wss\VirtualDirectories\17316\bin

I am not saying that you can not copy the assembly to the **_vti_bin** folder or **wwwroot** folder, of course you can but I have often seen people struggling with the service deployment. People often ask me where they should copy the assembly and what is the best place to put the assembly in. I tested my web service by putting the assembly file in all the recommended places and I found that **bin** folder of the virtual directory of the web application is the safest place where your web service is guaranteed to work.

Copy the assembly to the **bin** folder of the virtual directory of the web application of your choice. You will have to create the **bin** folder yourself. It is not there by default.

Adding web service to the GAC

30. You must add your assembly in the **GAC** on your SharePoint server. This is necessary otherwise you will get permissions error on the server. There are three ways to avoid this permissions error. One way is to add the assembly in the **GAC**. Second way is to change the trust level to **medium** in the web.config file and the third is to create a custom trust policy of your own. To learn about creating custom policies, see section on Code Access Security in this book.

To add your assembly to the **Global Assembly Cache (GAC)**, you can either drag and drop the assembly into the %windows%\assembly directory using 2 instances of Windows Explorer, or use the command line utility gacutil.exe that is installed with the .NET Framework SDK 2.0. This utility is located in the following folder:

C:\Program Files\Microsoft Visual Studio 8\SDK\v2.0\Bin

To use gacutil.exe to copy the class library DLL into the GAC

1. To open the Visual Studio command prompt, click **Start**, point to **All Programs**, point to **Microsoft Visual Studio 2005**, point to **Visual Studio Tools**, and click **Visual Studio 2005 Command Prompt**.

2. At the command prompt type a command in the following form, and press ENTER:

```
gacutil.exe -i "<Full file system path to DLL>"
```

Listing 7.12: *gacutil.exe utility*

TIP

You can also use ".NET Framework 2.0 Configuration" tool to add the assembly to the **GAC**.

1. Go to control panel, click **Administrative Tools** and select **Microsoft .NET Framework 2.0 Configuration**.

2. Click **Manage the Assembly Cache** and then select **Add an Assembly to the Assembly Cache**. Locate the assembly and click **Open**.

Creating a Windows Application to Consume the Web Service

After copying the Web services files to the **_vti_bin** directory, the next step is to create a Windows Application to consume the Web service.

31. Create a new C# Windows Application in Visual Studio 2005.

32. In **Solution Explorer**, right-click **References**, and then click **Add Web Reference**.

33. In the address bar of the **Add Web Reference** browser, type the URL for the site to which to apply the service, as follows, and then press ENTER:

http://localhost/_vti_bin/Files.asmx?wsdl

If you installed the service on another port, for example, port 17316, then the url would be:

http://localhost:17316/_vti_bin/Files.asmx?wsdl

You can also browse all web services available on the server. Files.asmx will be listed in the web services available on the server. There will be multiple entries, each entry representing the service available for a different web application. Therefore, if you want to upload documents to a site on port 80, then you should select Files.asmx for port 80.

34. Include following **using** directives at the top:

```
using System.Net;
using System.IO;
```

Listing 7.13: *Include namespaces*

35. Add following code to your application:

```
try
{
    localhost.Files oUploader = new localhost.Files();

    oUploader.PreAuthenticate = true;
    oUploader.Credentials = CredentialCache.DefaultCredentials;

    string strPath = @"C:\test.doc";
    string strFile = strPath.Substring(strPath.LastIndexOf("\\") + 1);

    string strDestination = "http://sp:17316/Docs";

    FileStream fStream = new FileStream(strPath, System.IO.FileMode.Open);
    byte[] binFile = new byte[(int)fStream.Length];
    fStream.Read(binFile, 0, (int)fStream.Length);
    fStream.Close();

    string str = oUploader.UploadDocument(strFile, binFile, strDestination);
    MessageBox.Show(str);
}
catch (Exception ex)
{
    MessageBox.Show(ex.Source + " - " + ex.Message + " - " + ex.InnerException + " - " +
ex.StackTrace);
}
```

Listing 7.14: *Consuming web service*

localhost is the name of the web reference that you added in previous step. **strPath** contains the filename that is to be uploaded. This is just a sample to show you how the service works, that's why i have hard coded the filename but in a real life situation you may want to add a text box and a browse button to select files from your hard disk. **strDestination** contains the destination path. This should be the path representing the document library where file is to be uploaded.

36. Finally, before testing the service, make sure the current user has privileges to upload documents in the destination document library. The user should have "Contributor" rights in the document library otherwise, you will get "401: Unauthorized" error. Run the application to test the service.

Frequently Asked Questions

Q: I get "Could not create type" error message. What could be the reason?

Make sure your .asmx file has correct class name definition. Open your .asmx file and if class name is **myFiles**, change it to **myService.myFiles**!

<%@ WebService Language="C#" Class="myService.myFiles" %> (Correct)

<%@ WebService Language="C#" Class="myFiles" %> (Incorrect)

It's better that you use correct format in the first place but you can change the .asmx file after deployment as well. Go to C:\Program Files\Common Files\Microsoft Shared\web server extensions\12\ISAPI folder and open your .asmx file in notepad (or any editor of your choice) and make the changes as mentioned above.

Q: I get "Server did not recognize the value of HTTP Header SOAPAction: ..." error?

This error occurs if you do not use correct web service namespace. Following three lines should be included in your code, just before the class defintion:

[WebService(Namespace = "http://tempuri.org/")]
[WebServiceBinding(ConformsTo = WsiProfiles.BasicProfile1_1)]
[ToolboxItem(false)]

This error can occur even if you omit the trailing slash of **http://tempuri.org/**, **http://tempuri.org** will result in an error.

Q: I get "File not found." error?

239

This happens when SharePoint fails to find the assembly file. Make sure you have added the assembly in the correct **bin** folder. Also, make sure you have added the assembly in the **GAC**.

Q: I get "Unauthorized" error?

Make sure the user who is trying to use the web service has "Contributor" rights in the destination site or library. Also, make sure following lines are added to your client application:

oUploader.PreAuthenticate = true;
oUploader.Credentials = CredentialCache.DefaultCredentials;

Q: I get "SQL Server might not be started" error. I have double checked, my SQL Server is running. Why am i getting the error?

There could be several reasons for this. If you modified the web.config file, reverse the changes you made to the config file and then try again. The error has nothing to do with the SQL Server.

Q: I do not see my web service when i click "Web services on the local machine" in **Add Web Reference**?

Did you make changes in the spsdisco.aspx file? To include your web service in the list of web services on the SharePoint server, you must add reference to your web service in the spsdisco.aspx file (within the discovery element).

Q: Is it necessary to include the code in the code-behind?

No! You can write code in the myFiles.asmx (markup page) and delete the myFiles.asmx.cs file. Here is the myFiles.asmx code listing:

```
<%@ WebService Language="C#" Class="myService.myFiles" %>

using System;
using System.Data;
using System.Web;
using System.Collections;
using System.Web.Services;
using System.Web.Services.Protocols;
using System.ComponentModel;
using Microsoft.SharePoint;
```

```
using Microsoft.SharePoint.WebControls;
using System.Net;

namespace myService
{
/// <summary>
/// Summary description for Service1
/// </summary>
[WebService(Namespace = "http://tempuri.org/")]
[WebServiceBinding(ConformsTo = WsiProfiles.BasicProfile1_1)]
[ToolboxItem(false)]
public class myFiles : System.Web.Services.WebService
{

//[WebMethod]
//public string HelloWorld()
//{
// return "Hello World";
//}
[WebMethod]
public string UploadDocument(string fileName, byte[] fileContents, string pathFolder)
{
if (fileContents == null)
{
return "Null Attachment";
}
try
{
int iStartIndex = pathFolder.LastIndexOf("/");
string sitePath = pathFolder.Remove(iStartIndex);
string folderName = pathFolder.Substring(iStartIndex + 1);

SPSite site = new SPSite(sitePath);
SPWeb web = site.OpenWeb();

SPFolder folder = web.GetFolder(folderName);

string fileURL = fileName;

folder.Files.Add(fileURL, fileContents);
```

```
if (folder.Files[fileURL].CheckedOutBy.Name != "")
{
folder.Files[fileURL].CheckIn("File Checked In");
}
return "File added successfully!";


}
catch (System.Exception ex)
{
return "Error: " + ex.Source + " - " + ex.Message;
}
}


}
}
```

Listing 7.15: *myFiles.asmx code*

SharePoint Programming Samples

Technoservice

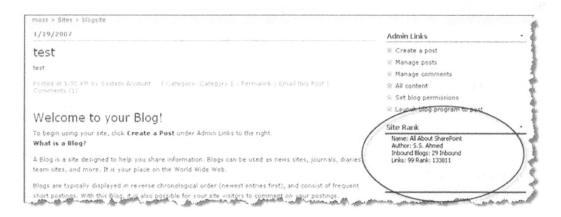

Figure 7.4: *Technoservice logo*

Now that you have learned how to create a custom web service for SharePoint, let's check out a web service that gets site or blog information from an external site. TechnoService is a web service that gets your site or blog information from Technorati (http://technorati.com/) using the Technorati API (http://technorati.com/developers/api/). This web service was written for MOSS 2007 and WSS 3.0.

Figure 7.5: *This is how the web service results look on a SharePoint page*

This functionality is also available in the form of a web part that will discuss later in another section.

The service returns a string that has following information:

1. Blog/Site Name
2. Author Name
3. Number of Inbound Blogs
4. Number of Inbound Links
5. Blog/Site Rank

Installation

1. Download files for this sample
(http://www.walisystems.com/articles/SPS/technoservice/1/DeployTechno.zip)

2. Unzip the downloaded file to a local folder on your machine (SharePoint server).

3. Copy the following files from the folder (where you unzipped the package) to the **_vti_bin** directory of the SharePoint server.

Techos.asmx
Technosdisco.aspx
Technoswsdl.aspx

The **_vti_bin** virtual directory maps physically to the Local_Drive:\Program Files\Common Files\Microsoft Shared\Web Server Extensions\12\ISAPI directory, which contains the default Web service files used in Windows SharePoint Services.

To include the Web service in the list of web services on the server

4. In Notepad, open the spsdisco.aspx file. spsdisco.aspx is located in the following directory (on the SharePoint server):

Local_Drive:\Program Files\Common Files\Microsoft Shared\web server extensions\12\ISAPI

5. Add the following lines to the end of the file within the discovery element (paste these lines just before the </discovery> element) and save the file:

Note: Please paste these lines to the notepad first to avoid copying the illegal characters or copy these lines from the spsdisco.aspx file that can be downloaded from the following link:

http://www.walisystems.com/articles/SPS/technoservice/1/spsdisco.zip (Compressed as zip file)

```
<contractRef ref=<%
SPHttpUtility.AddQuote(SPHttpUtility.HtmlEncode(spWeb.Url +
"/_vti_bin/Technos.asmx?wsdl"), Response.Output); %> docRef=<%
SPHttpUtility.AddQuote(SPHttpUtility.HtmlEncode(spWeb.Url +
"/_vti_bin/Technos.asmx"),
Response.Output); %> xmlns="http://schemas.xmlsoap.org/disco/scl/" />
<soap address=<% SPHttpUtility.AddQuote(SPHttpUtility.HtmlEncode(spWeb.Url +
"/_vti_bin/Technos.asmx"), Response.Output); %>
xmlns:q1="http://schemas.microsoft.com/sharepoint/soap/directory/"
binding="q1:TechnosSoap"
xmlns="http://schemas.xmlsoap.org/disco/soap/" />
```

Listing 7.16: *Modify spsdisco.aspx*

Copying the assembly to the Bin folder

6. Copy the **techno.dll** file to the **bin** folder of the default SharePoint web application. Following path contains the virtual directories of web applications that you have created on your SharePoint server.

Local_Drive:\Inetpub\wwwroot\wss\VirtualDirectories

If your default web application is configured at port 80 then you should copy the **techno.dll** file to the following folder:

Local_Drive:\Inetpub\wwwroot\wss\VirtualDirectories\80\bin

It is up to you, you may want to install the web service in some other application. For example, if you want to install it in an application configured at port 81, then copy the **techno.dll** to the following folder:

Local_Drive:\Inetpub\wwwroot\wss\VirtualDirectories\81\bin

Adding web service to the GAC

7. Go to following folder:

LocalDrive:\Program Files\Microsoft Visual Studio 8\SDK\v2.0\Bin and run the following command:

```
gacutil.exe -i "<Full file system path to Techno.DLL>"
```

Listing 7.17: *Run gacutil.exe*

Testing the Service

You can test the service in a windows application. Create a C# Windows application. Add a web reference to the web service that you just installed and use following code to test the service:

```csharp
private void Form1_Load(object sender, EventArgs e)
{
try
{
localhost.Technos o = new localhost.Technos();

MessageBox.Show(o.DoTechno(@"http://www.sharepointblogs.com/ssa",
"ec789b5b3ad9a6d0acd5e4a0d52591ee"));
}
catch (Exception ex)
{
MessageBox.Show(ex.Source + " - " + ex.Message + " - " + ex.InnerException + " - " +
ex.StackTrace);
}

}
```

Listing 7.18: *Testing the service*

DoTechno() method takes two arguments: url and key. Url is the url of the site or blog for which you want to retrieve the information and key is the key that is required to use the Technorati API. You can get the key by visiting the Technorati site. The code shown above will return following information:

Name: All About SharePoint
Author: S.S. Ahmed
Inbound Blogs: 29
Inbound Links: 99
Rank: 133811

OK

Figure 7.6: *Web service results*

I deployed this web service on my SharePoint blog site using the SharePoint designer. You can create a web part of your own to consume this web service, format the output by adding some style and display it anywhere in your SharePoint sites. The other method, as I said earlier, is to use the SharePoint designer.

Deploying the web service using SharePoint designer

1. Open a SharePoint site (Where you want to deploy the web service) in SharePoint designer.

2. Select **Manage Data Sources...** from the "Data View" menu. This will open the "Data Source Library" pane on the right side.

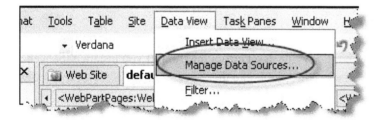

Figure 7.7: *Manage Data Sources...*

3. Expand the "XML Web Services" node and click **Connect to a web service**.

Figure 7.8: *Data Source Library*

4. Enter the web service reference in the **Service description location**. If you installed the web service in the root application then the path will look like this:

http://localhost/_vti_bin/technos.asmx?wsdl

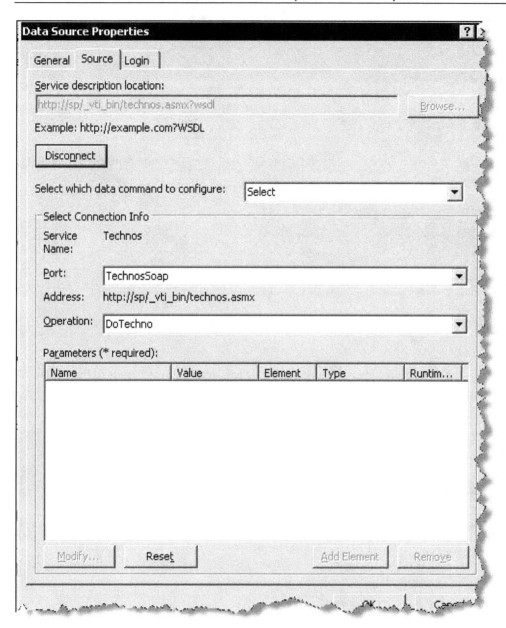

Figure 7.9: *Data Source Properties*

Leave all other options as they are and click the **OK** button.

5. Select **Insert Data View...** from the "Data View" menu. This will add a data view web part to the page.

Figure 7.10: *Insert Data View*

6. Click the link shown in the data view web part. This will open the **Data Sources Library** if it's not already open.

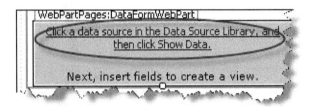

Figure 7.11: *Show data in web part*

7. Right click the web service that you added to the "XML Web Services" node in the "Data Sources Library" and click **Show Data**.

Figure 7.12: *Show Data*

Data returned from your web service will be displayed.

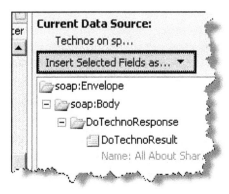

Figure 7.13: *Insert Selected Field as...*

8. Click the **Insert Selected Fields as...** drop down and select **Single Item View**.

9. That's it. Save the page and if you want to add some style to the data view web part, right click the data view web part and select **Modify > Table AutoFormat**. It will show you several options. Select the option of your choice and your data view web part is ready.

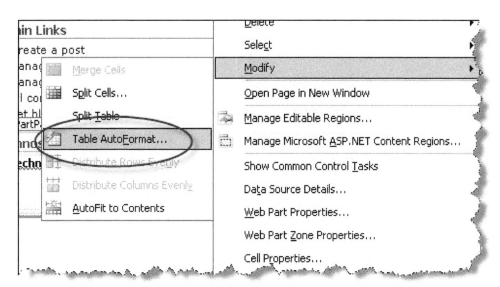

Figure 7.14: *Table AutoFormat*

You can apply formatting to the output returned by the web service manually as well. Anyway, here is how the data view web part looked in my SharePoint site after applying some styles:

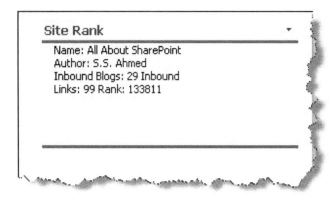

Figure 7.15: *Web service results using data view web part*

I changed the title and applied auto formatting.

Installing a web service

The WSUploadService that we created in the sections above is a web service that uploads documents from local file system to SharePoint. The web service comes with an installer and installing the web service on the server is a single-click process. When I first distributed this web service, I received a complaint from a couple of users who used non-English SharePoint and the complaint was that installation ended prematurely without installing the service successfully. I was not sure as to why the installation failed on the SharePoint server that was not using English as the main language but then I decided to write about it, the steps required to install web service manually. All these steps have also been explained above in the section that explained the web service creation process.

All you need are the files for the web service. You can download the files from the following link:

http://www.walisystems.com/articles/SPS/uplservice/v1/files.zip

1. Download the files from the above link.

2. Unzip the downloaded file to a local folder on your machine (SharePoint server).

3. Copy the following files from the folder (where you unzipped the package) to the _vti_bin directory of the SharePoint server.

```
Files.asmx
Filesdisco.aspx
Fileswsdl.aspx
```

Listing 7.19: *Files*

The _vti_bin virtual directory maps physically to the "Local_Drive:\Program Files\Common Files\Microsoft Shared\Web Server Extensions\12\ISAPI" directory, which contains the default Web service files used in Windows SharePoint Services.

To include the Web service in the list of web services on the server

4. In Notepad, open the spsdisco.aspx file. spsdisco.aspx is located in the following directory (on the SharePoint server):

Local_Drive:\Program Files\Common Files\Microsoft Shared\web server extensions\12\ISAPI

5. Add the following lines to the end of the file within the discovery element (paste these lines just before the </discovery> element) and save the file:

Note: Please paste these lines to the notepad first to avoid copying the illegal characters or copy these lines from the replacement.txt file (included in the zip package).

```
<contractRef ref=<% SPEncode.WriteHtmlEncodeWithQuote(Response, spWeb.Url +
"/_vti_bin/Files.asmx?wsdl",""); %> docRef=<%
SPEncode.WriteHtmlEncodeWithQuote(Response, spWeb.Url + "/_vti_bin/Files.asmx",
""); %> xmlns="http://schemas.xmlsoap.org/disco/scl/" />
<soap address=<% SPEncode.WriteHtmlEncodeWithQuote(Response, spWeb.Url +
"/_vti_bin/Files.asmx", ""); %>
xmlns:q1="http://schemas.microsoft.com/sharepoint/soap/directory/"
binding="q1:FilesSoap" xmlns="http://schemas.xmlsoap.org/disco/soap/" />
```

Listing 7.20: *spsdisco.aspx*

Copying the assembly to the Bin folder

6. Copy the UploadService.dll file to the bin folder of the default SharePoint web application. Following path contains the virtual directories of web applications that you have created on your SharePoint server.

Local_Drive:\Inetpub\wwwroot\wss\VirtualDirectories

If your default web application is configured at port 80 then you should copy the dll file to the following folder:

Local_Drive:\Inetpub\wwwroot\wss\VirtualDirectories\80

It is up to you, you may want to install the web service in some other application. For example, if you want to install it in an application configured at port 81, then copy the dll to the following folder:

Local_Drive:\Inetpub\wwwroot\wss\VirtualDirectories\81

Adding web service to the GAC

7. Go to following folder:

LocalDrive:\Program Files\Microsoft Visual Studio 8\SDK\v2.0\Bin

and run the following command:

```
gacutil.exe -i "<Full file system path to DLL>"
```

Listing 7.21: *gacutil.exe*

These were the steps to install a web service manually.

Creating installer for your web service

When I first wrote the installer for the WSUploadService (http://www.walisystems.com/ws1_dlc.asp), some people asked me how did I create the installer and then I started getting requests from people to share the installer code on regular basis. In this section, I will discuss the installer code.

This installer is a .NET application that copies the web service files to the correct folders on the destination machine. All manual work stated in the previous section is automatically done by the installer. After copying the files and modifying some of the default SharePoint files, installer application runs another installer package that simply copies the web service assembly to the correct bin folder. If you want to read about adding assembly to the GAC programmatically, here are two links that may be helpful:

Using the .NET Fusion API to Manipulate the GAC (http://www.codeguru.com/csharp/.net/net_general/assemblies/article.php/c12793)

Programmatically determining if a PIA is in the GAC (http://samgentile.com/blog/articles/2041.aspx)

Creating the second installer (to install assembly in the GAC) is very easy. Just create a web setup project, add the web service assembly file to the project, compile it and you are done. Of course, you may want to take some additional steps that are not actually required but can enhance the performance. For example, remove all dependency files from the package to reduce the installer size. Include a readme.txt in the package to let your users know about the installation steps, history, functionality, etc.

Create a C# application and add following namespaces at the top:

```
using System.IO;
using System.Diagnostics;
using Microsoft.Win32;
```

Listing 7.22: *Include namespaces*

Check Registry to see if the application is already installed. Ask the user if he wants to keep the application. Based on his response, take the action.

```
RegistryKey rk = Registry.LocalMachine;
RegistryKey nk = rk.OpenSubKey("SOFTWARE\\UploadService");
bool bGoAhead = false;

DialogResult response;

if (nk == null)
{
bGoAhead = true;
}
else
{
if ((string)nk.GetValue("Installed") == "1")
{
response = MessageBox.Show("UploadService is already installed! Do you want to
uninstall?", "Uninstall", MessageBoxButtons.YesNo, MessageBoxIcon.Question);
```

Listing 7.23: *Modifying registry*

If the response from the user is Yes, that is, if he wants to continue with the uninstall, run the following code:

```
if (response == DialogResult.Yes)
{
//Uninstall
string dest = (string)nk.GetValue("Path") + @"Program Files\Common Files\Microsoft
Shared\web server extensions\12\ISAPI\";

if (File.Exists(dest + "Files.asmx"))
{
File.Delete(dest + "Files.asmx");
}
if (File.Exists(dest + "Filesdisco.aspx"))
{
File.Delete(dest + "Filesdisco.aspx");
}
if (File.Exists(dest + "Fileswsdl.aspx"))
{
```

```
File.Delete(dest + "Fileswsdl.aspx");
}
if (File.Exists(dest + "spsdisco_backup.aspx"))
{
File.Delete(dest + "spsdisco.aspx");
File.Copy(dest + "spsdisco_backup.aspx", dest + "spsdisco.aspx");
File.Delete(dest + "spsdisco_backup.aspx");
}
RegistryKey regkey = Registry.LocalMachine;
RegistryKey newkey = regkey.CreateSubKey("SOFTWARE\\UploadService");
newkey.SetValue("Installed", "0");

//MessageBox.Show("Uninstall");
System.Diagnostics.Process.Start(Environment.CurrentDirectory + "\\setup.exe");

//bGoAhead = true;
this.Close();
```

Listing 7.24: *Run setup.exe*

This code will remove the values from the registry and then invoke the setup.exe (the second installer) which will remove the web service assembly from the GAC.

If he cancels the setup, simply close the application.

```
else
{
bGoAhead = false;
this.Close();
}
```

Listing 7.25: *Close application*

If the user is running the setup for the first time to install the web service, then use the following code to add values to the registry and run the second installer:

```
string[] drives = Environment.GetLogicalDrives();
string sPath = @"Program Files\Common Files\Microsoft Shared\web server
extensions\12\ISAPI\";


foreach (string sDrive in drives)
{
if (System.IO.Directory.Exists(sDrive + sPath))
{

if ((File.Exists(Environment.CurrentDirectory + "\\Files.asmx") && (!File.Exists(sDrive +
sPath + "Files.asmx"))))
{
installed = true;
File.Copy(Environment.CurrentDirectory + "\\Files.asmx", sDrive + sPath + "Files.asmx",
true);

//Modify spsdisco.aspx file!
Modify(sDrive + sPath,"spsdisco",".aspx");


}
if ((File.Exists(Environment.CurrentDirectory + "\\Filesdisco.aspx") &&
(!File.Exists(sDrive + sPath + "Filesdisco.aspx"))))
{
File.Copy(Environment.CurrentDirectory + "\\Filesdisco.aspx", sDrive + sPath +
"Filesdisco.aspx", true);
}
if ((File.Exists(Environment.CurrentDirectory + "\\Fileswsdl.aspx") &&
(!File.Exists(sDrive + sPath + "Fileswsdl.aspx"))))
{
File.Copy(Environment.CurrentDirectory + "\\Fileswsdl.aspx", sDrive + sPath +
"Fileswsdl.aspx", true);
}
if (!installed)
{
MessageBox.Show("UploadService could not be installed because default SharePoint
installation directory could not be found. Make sure SharePoint is installed on this
machine.");
this.Close();
```

```
}


System.Diagnostics.Process.Start(Environment.CurrentDirectory + "\\setup.exe");


//MessageBox.Show("UploadService has been installed successfully!");
RegistryKey regkey = Registry.LocalMachine;
RegistryKey newkey = regkey.CreateSubKey("SOFTWARE\\UploadService");
newkey.SetValue("Installed", "1");
newkey.SetValue("Path", sDrive.ToString());
//break;
this.Close();
```

Listing 7.26: *Add values to registry and run second installer*

The above code uses a Modify() function. Modify() function modifies the spsdisco.aspx file and includes the reference to the web service being installed. After this, the web service will become visible to the users searching for the web services on the server. Here is the Modify() code:

```
public void Modify(string spsPath, string filename, string ext)
{
try
{
File.Copy(spsPath + filename + ext, spsPath + filename + "_backup" + ext);
File.Delete(spsPath + filename + ext);

StreamReader sr,sr1;
StreamWriter sw;

sw = File.CreateText(spsPath + filename + ext);
sr1 = File.OpenText(Environment.CurrentDirectory + "\\replacement.txt");
string str2 = sr1.ReadLine();
string str1 = string.Empty;

while (str2 != null)
{
str1 += str2;
```

```
str2 = sr1.ReadLine();
}

sr = File.OpenText(spsPath + filename + "_backup" + ext);
string str = sr.ReadLine();

while (str!=null)
{
if (str.Substring(0) == "</discovery>")
{
str = str.Replace("</discovery>", str1);
}

sw.WriteLine(str);
str = sr.ReadLine();
}

sr.Close();
sr1.Close();
sw.Close();

}
catch (Exception ex)
{
MessageBox.Show(ex.Source + " - " + ex.Message + " - Could not modify the
spsdisco.aspx file. Contact web service vendor!");
}
}
```

Listing 7.27: *Modify function*

This function copies the content of replacement.txt to the spsdisco.aspx file. The code automatically makes a backup copy of the spsdisco.aspx file so that you can go back to the original settings if required. Replacement.txt contains the following:

```
<contractRef ref=<% SPEncode.WriteHtmlEncodeWithQuote(Response, spWeb.Url +
"/_vti_bin/Files.asmx?wsdl",""); %> docRef=<%
SPEncode.WriteHtmlEncodeWithQuote(Response, spWeb.Url + "/_vti_bin/Files.asmx",
""); %> xmlns="http://schemas.xmlsoap.org/disco/scl/" />
```

```
<soap address=<% SPEncode.WriteHtmlEncodeWithQuote(Response, spWeb.Url +
"/_vti_bin/Files.asmx", ""); %>
xmlns:q1="http://schemas.microsoft.com/sharepoint/soap/directory/"
binding="q1:FilesSoap" xmlns="http://schemas.xmlsoap.org/disco/soap/" />

</discovery>
```

Listing 7.28: *spsdisco.aspx*

Download the installer code from the following link:

http://www.walisystems.com/articles/SPS/uplservice/v1/installer/UploadServiceCopier.zip

Download size is 414 KB.

To download the installer application that installs web service assembly to the GAC, visit following link:

http://www.walisystems.com/articles/SPS/uplservice/v1/installer/Setup.zip

Download size is 358 KB.

Technopart

TechnoPart is a web part that gets site or blog information from Technorati (http://technorati.com/). It uses the Technorati API (http://technorati.com/developers/api/). Download this web part from the following link:

http://www.walisystems.com/techno_dlc.asp

Technopart installation

Figure 7.16: *Technopart in action*

The TechnoPart retrieves following information from the Technorati site:

1. Blog/Site Name
2. Author Name
3. Rank
4. Inbound Blogs
5. Inbound Links

Following are the steps required to install TechnoPart on your server:

1. Copy the Technocab.CAB file to the following location on the server:

263

C:\Program Files\Common Files\Microsoft Shared\web server extensions\12\bin

This location also contains stsadm.exe file.

3.   From the location mentioned in Step 1, run the following command:

```
stsadm -o addwppack -filename Technocab.CAB -url http://localhost -globalinstall -force
```

Listing 7.29: *stsadm command line utility*

(Change localhost to your servername. You can install it anywhere including the root site.)

3. Run following command to reset IIS:

```
iisreset /timeout:0
```

Listing 7.30: *Reset IIS*

4. To add TechnoPart to the SharePoint site, open the site in a web browser.

5. Click **Site Actions** and select **Edit Page**.

Figure 7.17: *Edit page*

6. Click **Add a Web Part** (in Right zone).

7. Expand **All Web Parts** by clicking the + button.

8. Select **WS-TechnoPart** from the **Miscellaneous** section.

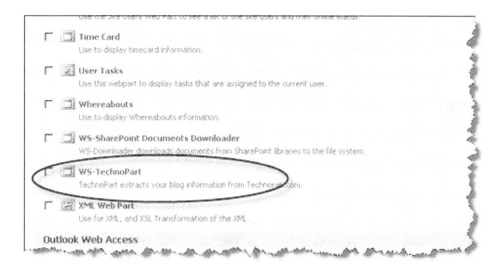

Figure 7.18: *Select web part*

9. Click the **Publish** button to publish the changes.

Figure 7.19: *Publish changes*

10. Now, test the web part by refreshing the page where you added the part. By default, it will show you my blog's (http://www.sharepointblogs.com/ssa) stats. You can change the blog/site URL. Here are the steps:

11. Click the arrow at the top right corner of the TechnoPart and select "Modify Shared Web Part".

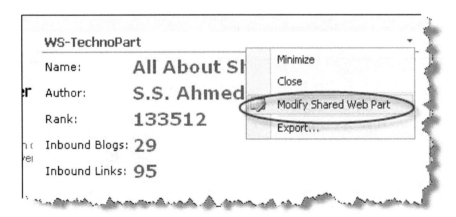

Figure 7.20: *Blog stats*

12. Expand the "Miscellaneous" section by clicking the + sign and enter the URL of the site or blog for which you want to retrieve information in the **Site URL** box. By default, **Site URL** contains my blog's URL (http://www.sharepointblogs.com/ssa). Enter Technorati Key

(http://technorati.com/developers/apikey.html) in the **Technorati Key** box. This key is required to get information from the Technorati site using the API (http://technorati.com/developers/api/). To get a key for your own site or blog, visit Technorati site. You can use this key to get information for any blog or site registered on Technorati which means that even if you do not change the default value in the **Technorati Key** box, you will still be able to retrieve information from the Technorati site.

Figure 7.21: *Change web part settings*

Remove TechnoPart

Following are the instructions to remove TechnoPart from your server:

1. Go to following location on the server:

C:\Program Files\Common Files\Microsoft Shared\web server extensions\12\bin

2. Run following command to remove the web part.

```
stsadm -o deletewppack -name Technocab.cab -url http://localhost
```

Listing 7.31: *Remove web part*

(Change localhost to your servername.)

Examples

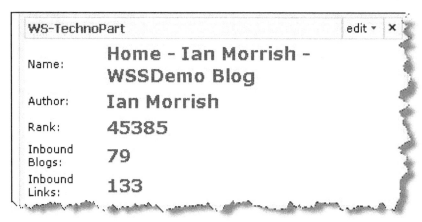

Figure 7.22: *Ian Morrish's blog stats*

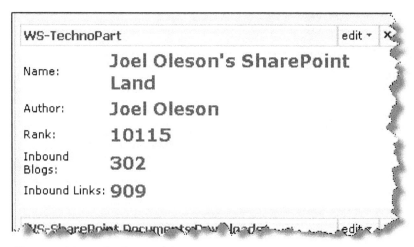

Figure 7.23: *Joel Oleson's blog stats*

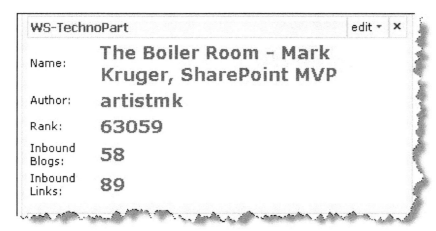

Figure 7.24: *Mark Kruger's blog stats*

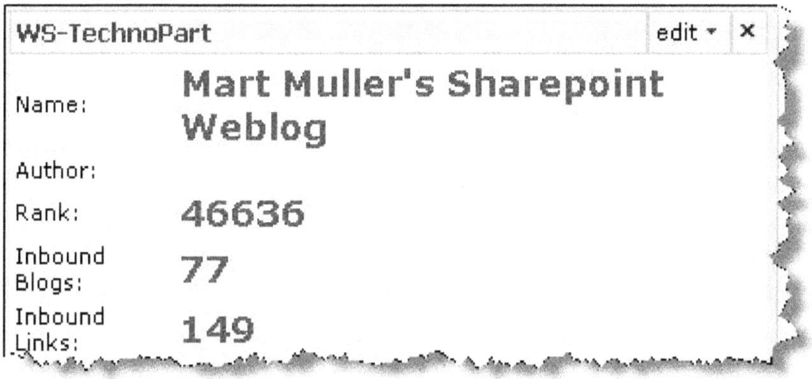

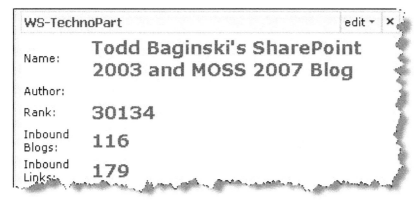

Figure 7.25: *Mart Muller's blog stats*

Figure 7.26: *Todd Baginski's blog stats*

Download complete application (source code) from the following link:

http://www.walisystems.com/technocode_dlc.asp

Let's look at the code of this web part.

Development Environment: MOSS 2007, .NET Framework 2.0, VS 2005
Programming Language: C#

Download and unzip TechnoPart.zip (http://www.walisystems.com/technocode_dlc.asp) file on your hard disk.

It will create a folder **TechnoPart.** There will be two folders (projects) inside this **TechnoPart** folder:

1. **Technocab** -> This is the setup project.
2. **WS-DLWP** -> This is the web part project.

And there is a **WS-DLWP.sln** solution file along with these two folders. Double click this solution file to open the project in Visual Studio 2005.

GetSiteData() is the function that connects with Technorati (http://www.technorati.com/) through the API (http://www.technorati.com/developers/api/).

```
Public void GetSiteData ()
{

BuildUrl();

string strURL = apiUrl + "bloginfo?" + queryString;

try
{

XmlTextReader _reader = new XmlTextReader(strURL.ToString());

//Read elements

while (_reader.Read())
```

```
{
if (_reader.NodeType == XmlNodeType.Element && _reader.Name == "rank")
{
_lblRank.Text = _reader.ReadElementString("rank");
}
else if (_reader.NodeType == XmlNodeType.Element && _reader.Name ==
"inboundblogs")
{
_lblBlogs.Text = _reader.ReadElementString("inboundblogs");
}
else if (_reader.NodeType == XmlNodeType.Element && _reader.Name ==
"inboundlinks")
{
_lblLinks.Text = _reader.ReadElementString("inboundlinks");
}
else if (_reader.NodeType == XmlNodeType.Element && _reader.Name == "name")
{
_lblName.Text = _reader.ReadElementString("name");
}
else if (_reader.NodeType == XmlNodeType.Element && _reader.Name == "firstname")
{
_lblAuthor.Text = _reader.ReadElementString("firstname");
}
else if (_reader.NodeType == XmlNodeType.Element && _reader.Name == "lastname")
{
_lblAuthor.Text = _lblAuthor.Text + " " + _reader.ReadElementString("lastname");
}
}

//Close the XML reader
_reader.Close();
}

catch (WebException ex)
{
_lblError.Text = ex.Message;
_lblError.CssClass = "error";
}
```

Listing 7.32: *GetSiteData() code*

Add a style to the web part:

```
//Create a stylesheet
HtmlGenericControl stylesheet = new HtmlGenericControl("style");
stylesheet.InnerHtml = ReplaceTokens(Constants.Styles);
this.Controls.Add(stylesheet);
```

Listing 7.33: *Add style to web part*

Build the interface:

```
// Build up the table that is our user interface.
Table t = new Table();
TableRow trRank = BuildTableRow();
TableRow trBlogs = BuildTableRow();
TableRow trLinks = BuildTableRow();
TableRow trError = BuildTableRow();
TableRow trName = BuildTableRow();
TableRow trAuthor = BuildTableRow();

trName.Cells[0].Text = "Name: ";
trName.Cells[1].ForeColor = System.Drawing.Color.Green;
trName.Cells[1].Font.Bold = true;
trName.Cells[1].Font.Size = FontUnit.Medium;
trName.Cells[1].Controls.Add(_lblName);

trAuthor.Cells[0].Text = "Author: ";
trAuthor.Cells[1].ForeColor = System.Drawing.Color.Green;
trAuthor.Cells[1].Font.Bold = true;
trAuthor.Cells[1].Font.Size = FontUnit.Medium;
trAuthor.Cells[1].Controls.Add(_lblAuthor);

trRank.Cells[0].Text = "Rank: ";
trRank.Cells[1].ForeColor = System.Drawing.Color.Green;
trRank.Cells[1].Font.Bold = true;
trRank.Cells[1].Font.Size = FontUnit.Medium;
trRank.Cells[1].Controls.Add(_lblRank);
```

```
trBlogs.Cells[0].Text = "Inbound Blogs: ";
trBlogs.Cells[1].ForeColor = System.Drawing.Color.Green;
trBlogs.Cells[1].Font.Bold = true;
trBlogs.Cells[1].Font.Size = FontUnit.Medium;
trBlogs.Cells[1].Controls.Add(_lblBlogs);

trLinks.Cells[0].Text = "Inbound Links: ";
trLinks.Cells[1].ForeColor = System.Drawing.Color.Green;
trLinks.Cells[1].Font.Bold = true;
trLinks.Cells[1].Font.Size = FontUnit.Medium;
trLinks.Cells[1].Controls.Add(_lblLinks);

trError.Cells[0].Text = "";
trError.Cells[1].Controls.Add(_lblError);

t.Rows.AddRange(new TableRow[]{
trName,
trAuthor,
trRank,
trBlogs,
trLinks,
trError
});

this.Controls.Add(t);
```

Listing 7.34: *Build interface*

Download complete application (Source code):

http://www.walisystems.com/technocode_dlc.asp

WS-Downloader

WS-Downloader is a small tool that downloads documents from SharePoint libraries. There is a room for improvement in the tool. Currently, it's in a very basic form having two text boxes, one for the document library path and the other for entering the destination path on the local computer.

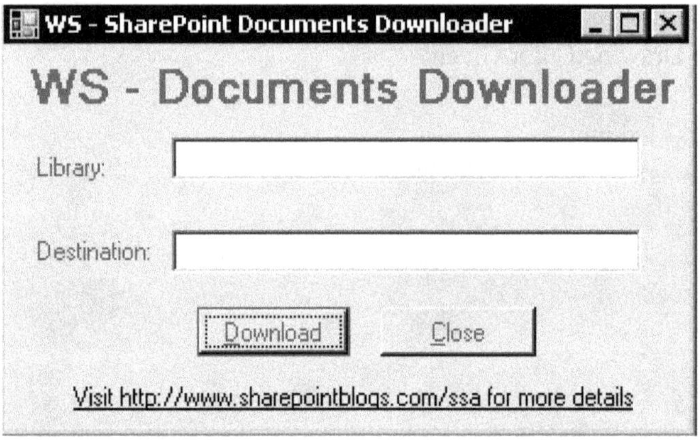

Figure 7.27: *Downloading tool*

Usage

Enter document library path in the first text box, for example, *http://portal/sitedirectory/site1/doclib1*.

Enter local path in the **Destination** box, for example, *C:\My Documents\Store*

Click the **Download** button to start downloading documents.

It will download all documents from the library to the local file system.

To Do

1. It currently works on the server machine. You will have to use it on the SharePoint server machine. To make it work remotely, write a web service which will make downloading documents remotely possible.

2. Instead of entering library path manually, there should be a drop down or a list box with check boxes for users to select the library.

3. It can not maintain the folder structure while downloading the files from the library. It will download the files from the root of the library as well as folders inside the library but the folder structure won't be copied to the file system. For example, if there are two files in the library and 2 files in the folder inside the library, the tool will download 4 files in total but without creating the folder on the file system.

Download

Click following link to download the zip file. Zip file contains only the .exe.

http://www.walisystems.com/articles/SPS/downloader/v1/ws-downloader.zip

WS-Downloader Web Part

The download tool we saw in the previous section is also available as a web part.

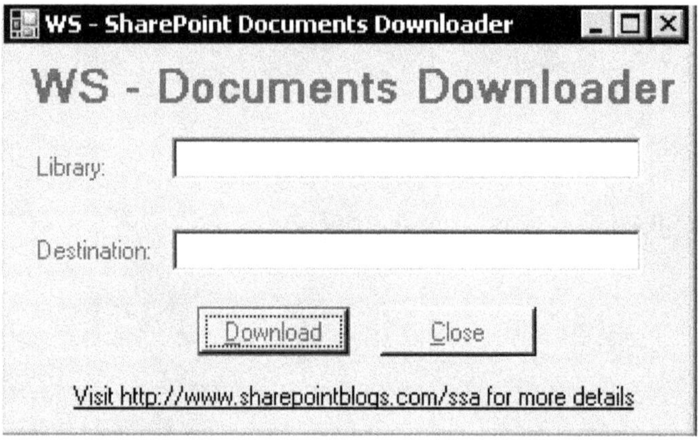

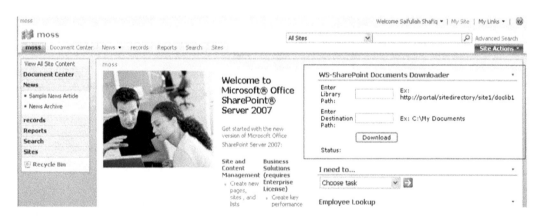

Figure 7.28: *Downloading tool*

You can plug this web part directly in any of your sites.

Figure 7.29: *Web part in action*

Click following link to download the web part cab file:

http://www.walisystems.com/articles/SPS/downloader/wp/v1/wsdlcab.CAB

Installation Instructions

1. Copy the wsdlcab.CAB file to the following location on the server:

C:\Program Files\Common Files\Microsoft Shared\web server extensions\12\bin

This location also contains stsadm.exe file.

2. From the location mentioned in Step 1, run the following command:

```
stsadm -o addwppack -filename wsdlcab.CAB -url http://localhost -globalinstall -force
```

Listing 7.35: *Install web part*

(Change localhost to your servername.)

3. Run following command to reset IIS:

```
iisreset /timeout:0
```

Listing 7.37: *Reset IIS*

4. Now, add the web part to a SharePoint site. Open the SharePoint site in a web browser.

5. Click **Site Actions** and select **Edit Page**.

Figure 7.30: *Edit page*

6. Click **Add a Web Part** (in Right zone).

7. Expand **All Web Parts** by clicking the + button.

8. Select **WS-SharePoint Documents Downloader** from the **Miscellaneous** section.

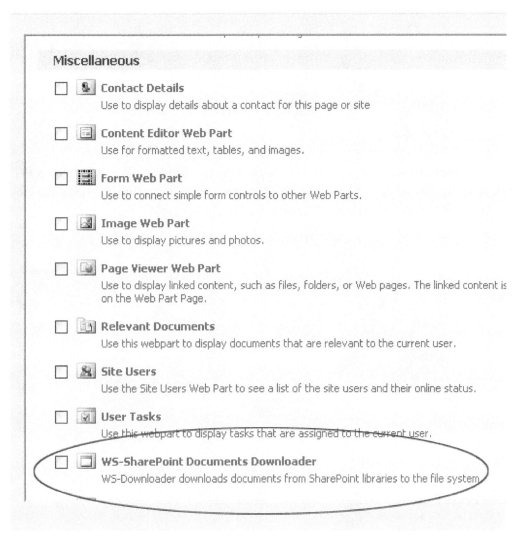

Figure 7.31: *Add web part*

9. Click the **Publish** button to publish the changes.

Figure 7.32: *Publish changes*

10. Now, test the web part by entering a library path in the first text box and a destination path in the second text box and clicking the **Download** button. This will download the documents to the destination folder and a message will be displayed in the web part.

Figure 7.33: *Web part in action*

Delete Web Part

1. Go to following location on the server:

C:\Program Files\Common Files\Microsoft Shared\web server extensions\12\bin

2. Run following command to remove the web part.

```
stsadm -o deletewppack -name wsdlcab.cab -url http://localhost
```

Listing 7.38: *Delete web part*

(Change localhost to your servername.)

Advantage

Now, you can run the application remotely and save the files to a local folder on the server. Remember, you still can not save the files to the client machine. For that, we need to write a web service and run the download application locally. To download the files to a folder on the server from a client machine, open the site in a web browser on the client machine. Select source and destination paths and click the **Download** button.

MOSS 2007 Upload Tool

I created this tool for MOSS 2007 when its first beta was released. There was so much craze for this product. People were busy exploring the product. I wrote this application for demo and my readers really liked this small tool although it was meant for demo only. It's a good small application for learning object model programming. The tool uploads files from your machine to the SharePoint server.

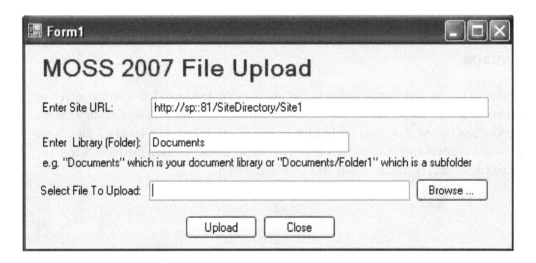

Figure 7.34: *MOSS 2007 File Upload Tool*

Download this application from following link:

http://walisystems.com/articles/SPS/mossupl/mossupl.rar

Creating list definition and WSP for a SharePoint list

This chapter has grown quite big. In this section, you will see how a WSP for a SharePoint list is created. Create a WSP for your SharePoint list in few simple steps. This is not a new topic and has already been written about. Following are some popular links that you may find useful:
Creating a SharePoint Solution Package (.WSP) in five steps
(http://geekswithblogs.net/evgenyblog/archive/2008/01/27/118966.aspx)

WSPBuilder Tool
(http://www.codeplex.com/wspbuilder)

Creating a Solution Package in Windows SharePoint Services 3.0
(http://msdn.microsoft.com/en-us/library/bb466225.aspx)

Creating and Deploying SharePoint Solution Files
(http://www.devx.com/dotnet/Article/40007/1954)

We will use "SharePoint Solution Generator" to create the WSP. "SharePoint Solution Generator" is a free utility that comes with the Visual Studio Extensions. You can download Visual Studio 2008 extensions from the following link:

http://www.microsoft.com/downloads/details.aspx?familyid=7BF65B28-06E2-4E87-9BAD-086E32185E68&displaylang=en

You can download Visual Studio 2005 Extensions from the following link:

http://www.microsoft.com/downloads/details.aspx?FamilyId=5D61409E-1FA3-48CF-8023-E8F38E709BA6&displaylang=en

I will use Visual Studio 2005 Extensions.

1. Start "SharePoint Solution Generator".

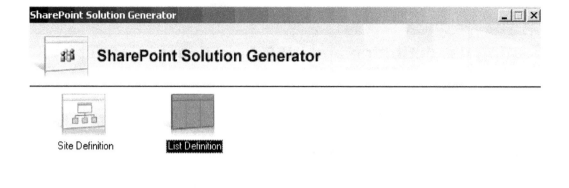

Figure 7.35: *SharePoint Solution Generator*

2. Select "List Definition" and click "Next".

3. Choose the site where the list is located. If you know the site URL, select the second option "Specify a site url:" and then enter the site URL and click "Next".

4. Select the list from the available lists and click "Next".

5. Enter a project name and select the location to save the project. Click "Next".

6. Click "Finish" to start the list generation.

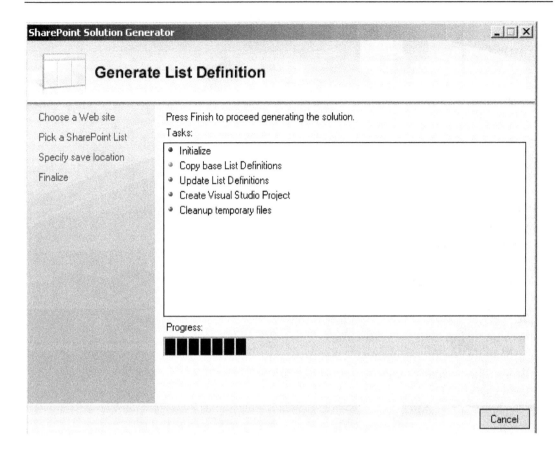

Figure 7.36: *List generation in progress*

7. Click the link "Click here to open the generated solution" to open the project or click the "Exit" button to close the wizard.

8. Double click the .csproj file to open the project in Visual Studio.

9. You need to add following three files in the project:

a. Instance.xml
b. Element.xml
c. Feature.xml

I have created a utility that creates these three files. That utility will not be included with this book. I will publish it on my blog soon. Keep visiting my blog for updated information:
http://vspug.com/ssa

285

Feature.xml

```xml
<?xml version="1.0" encoding="utf-8"?>
<Feature Id="06D1DF7A-3D3F-49b6-9388-74B8F26B50F2"
Title="MyList"
Description="MyList List Definition"
Version="1.0.0.0"
Scope="Web"
Hidden="FALSE"
DefaultResourceFile="MyList"
xmlns="http://schemas.microsoft.com/sharepoint/">
<ElementManifests>
<ElementManifest Location="Element.xml" />
<ElementFile Location="MyList\schema.xml" />
<ElementFile Location="MyList\AllItems.aspx" />
<ElementFile Location="MyList\DispForm.aspx" />
<ElementFile Location="MyList\EditForm.aspx" />
<ElementFile Location="MyList\NewForm.aspx" />
<ElementManifest Location="MyList\instance.xml"/>
</ElementManifests>
</Feature>
```

Listing 7.39: *Feature.xml*

Change the "Feature Id". Use "Create GUID" tool in Visual Studio to create the new GUID for the feature Id. Change the "Title" and "Description". If you are copying and pasting above XML, then replace "MyList" (wherever it is used) with your list's name.

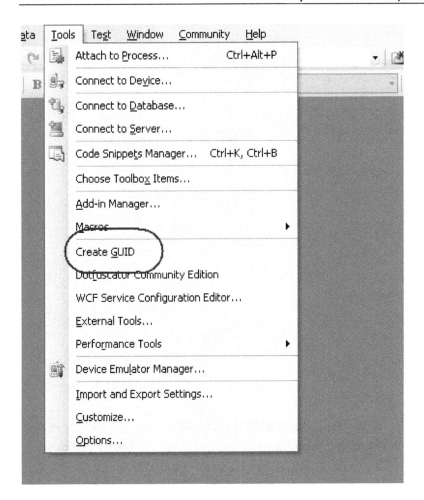

Figure 7.37: *Create GUID Tool in Visual Studio*

Element.xml

```xml
<?xml version="1.0" encoding="utf-8"?>
<Elements xmlns="http://schemas.microsoft.com/sharepoint/">
<ListTemplate
Name="MyList"
Type="10000"
BaseType="0"
OnQuickLaunch="TRUE"
SecurityBits="11"
Hidden="TRUE"
DisplayName="MyList"
Description="MyList List Definition"
Image=""/>
</Elements>
```

Listing 7.40: *Element.xml*

Change the name from "MyList" to your list's name. "Type" should unique. You can use any number, condition is it should be unique. Also, change "DisplayName" and "Description".

Instance.xml

```
<?xml version="1.0" encoding="utf-8"?>
<Elements xmlns="http://schemas.microsoft.com/sharepoint/">
<ListInstance
FeatureId="06D1DF7A-3D3F-49b6-9388-74B8F26B50F2"
TemplateType="10000"
Title="MyList"
Description="MyList instance"
OnQuickLaunch="false"
Url="Lists/MyList">

</ListInstance>
</Elements>
```

Listing 7.41: *Instance.xml*

Copy "FeatureId" from the "Feature.xml". "TemplateType" is the unique number that you used in Element.xml also. This is the template type and should always be unique. Change "Title", "Description" and "Url".

If you want to show data in your list, it is this file "Instance.xml" where you include your data. Use following Instance.xml if you want to include data:

Instance.xml (with data)

```
<?xml version="1.0" encoding="utf-8"?>
<Elements xmlns="http://schemas.microsoft.com/sharepoint/">
<ListInstance
FeatureId="06D1DF7A-3D3F-49b6-9388-74B8F26B50F2"
TemplateType="10000"
Title="MyList"
Description="MyList instance"
OnQuickLaunch="false"
Url="Lists/MyList">

<Data>
<Rows>
```

```
<Row>
<Field Name="YOUR FIELD NAME">My Value</Field>
<Field Name='ID'>1</Field>
</Row>

</Rows>
</Data>

</ListInstance>
</Elements>
```

Listing 7.42: *Instance.xml (with data)*

Add all fields with their values inside "<Data><Rows><Row>" and "</Row></Rows></Data>" tags.

10. If you are using latest version of Solution Generator, then you may not face this issue but old version of Solution Generator adds an extra line of code in the generated files, which causes problems when the list is rendered in SharePoint. So check your files and remove this redundant line if it is there. For example, open "AllItems.aspx" and if it has the following line (Remember, it will be a commented line) at the top, remove it:

```
<!-- _filecategory="ListDefinition" _filetype="File" _filename="AllItems.aspx"
_uniqueid="c6101d3b-569f-4f42-ab91-ff241ebbb439" -->
```

Listing 7.43: *Remove commented line from the top*

Save and close "AllItems.aspx".

11. Open "DispForm.aspx" and remove the following line from the top and save the file:

```
<!-- _filecategory="ListDefinition" _filetype="File" _filename="DispForm.aspx"
_uniqueid="bb83bef0-619f-4742-9314-7ec4efcb4631" -->
```

Listing 7.44: *Remove commented line from the top*

12. Open "EditForm.aspx" and remove the following line from the top and save the file:

```
<!-- _filecategory="ListDefinition" _filetype="File" _filename="EditForm.aspx"
_uniqueid="ef8f4a9d-7109-42bb-a966-fe8e9b13f63a" -->
```

Listing 7.45: *Remove commented line from the top*

13. Open "NewForm.aspx" file and remove following line from the top and save the file:

```
<!-- _filecategory="ListDefinition" _filetype="File" _filename="NewForm.aspx"
_uniqueid="a4917934-bc03-4c64-99c6-f2d68cebb087" -->
```

Listing 7.46: *Remove commented line from the top*

14. Open "Schema.xml" file and remove following line (It will be the second line):

```
<!-- _filecategory="ListDefinition" _filetype="Schema" _filename="schema.xml"
_uniqueid="96557fd3-f461-464a-9c7a-fb09f8598cea" -->
```

Listing 7.47: *Remove commented line from the top*

Change the value in the "Type" attribute of the <List> tag. This will be the first line in the code. Change the value to the unique template Id that you used in Element.xml and Instance.xml. The line will look like as following after the change:

```
<List Title="Announcements" Description="Use the Announcements list to post messages
on the home page of your site." Direction="0" BaseType="0" Url="Lists/Announcements"
FolderCreation="FALSE" Version="0" Type="10000"
xmlns="http://schemas.microsoft.com/sharepoint/">
```

Listing 7.48: *List definition*

291

Save the file.

15. Add a new folder called "Solution" in the project. Add two files "cab.ddf" and "manifest.xml" in the folder. Add a folder called "Package" in the "Solution" folder and add a file "Setup.bat" in it.

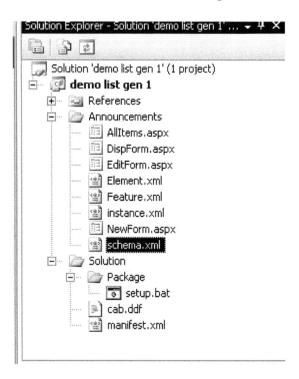

Figure 7.38: *Folder structure*

16. Here is manifest.xml:

Manifest.xml

```
<Solution
SolutionId="53571E0D-0240-427e-AB0E-2412D0729C5C"
xmlns="http://schemas.microsoft.com/sharepoint/" >
<FeatureManifests>
<FeatureManifest Location="MyList\feature.xml" />
</FeatureManifests>
```

</Solution>

Listing 7.49: *Manifest.xml*

Create new GUID for the "SolutionId".

17. cab.ddf should look like the following:

cab.ddf

```
; ** MyList.wsp **
.OPTION EXPLICIT ; Generate errors
.Set CabinetNameTemplate=MyList.wsp
.set DiskDirectoryTemplate=CDROM ; All cabinets go in a single directory
.Set CompressionType=MSZIP ; ** All files are compressed in cabinet files
.Set UniqueFiles="ON"
.Set Cabinet=on
.Set DiskDirectory1=Solution\Package
Solution\manifest.xml manifest.xml

MyList\Feature.xml MyList\Feature.xml
MyList\Element.xml MyList\Element.xml

MyList\instance.xml MyList\MyList\instance.xml
MyList\AllItems.aspx MyList\MyList\AllItems.aspx
MyList\DispForm.aspx MyList\MyList\DispForm.aspx
MyList\EditForm.aspx MyList\MyList\EditForm.aspx
MyList\NewForm.aspx MyList\MyList\NewForm.aspx
MyList\schema.xml MyList\MyList\schema.xml


bin\Debug\MyList.dll MyList.dll
; ** end **
```

Listing 7.50: *cab.ddf*

18. Copy following code and paste in the "setup.bat":

setup.bat

```
@rem=======================================
@rem
@rem setup.bat
@rem
@rem=======================================

@echo off
setlocal
pushd .

goto LInitialize

@rem-----------------------------------------------------------
@rem LInitialize
@rem-----------------------------------------------------------
:LInitialize
set SPAdminTool=%CommonProgramFiles%\Microsoft Shared\web server
extensions\12\BIN\stsadm.exe
set Install=
set Uninstall=
set PackageFile=%~dp0MyList.wsp
set PackageName=MyList.wsp
set DefaultWebUrl=http://myserver/
set DefaultSiteUrl=http://myserver/
set TargetWebUrl=
set TargetSiteUrl=

goto LParseArgs

@rem-----------------------------------------------------------
@rem LParseArgs
@rem-----------------------------------------------------------
:LParseArgs
```

```
@rem --- help ---
if "%1" == "/?" goto LHelp
if "%1" == "-?" goto LHelp
if "%1" == "/h" goto LHelp
if "%1" == "-h" goto LHelp
if "%1" == "/help" goto LHelp
if "%1" == "-help" goto LHelp


@rem --- Fix execute task ---
if "%1" == "/i" (set Install=1) & shift & goto LParseArgs
if "%1" == "-i" (set Install=1) & shift & goto LParseArgs
if "%1" == "/install" (set Install=1) & shift & goto LParseArgs
if "%1" == "-install" (set Install=1) & shift & goto LParseArgs
if "%1" == "/u" (set Uninstall=1) & shift & goto LParseArgs
if "%1" == "-u" (set Uninstall=1) & shift & goto LParseArgs
if "%1" == "/uninstall" (set Uninstall=1) & shift & goto LParseArgs
if "%1" == "-uninstall" (set Uninstall=1) & shift & goto LParseArgs


@rem --- Fix url ---
if "%1" == "/weburl" (set TargetWebUrl=%2) & shift & shift & goto LParseArgs
if "%1" == "-weburl" (set TargetWebUrl=%2) & shift & shift & goto LParseArgs
if "%1" == "/siteurl" (set TargetSiteUrl=%2) & shift & shift & goto LParseArgs
if "%1" == "-siteurl" (set TargetSiteUrl=%2) & shift & shift & goto LParseArgs

@rem --- Check invalid arguments ---
if not "%1" == "" (
echo Invalid argument.
goto LHelp
)


@rem --- Check arguments ---
if "%Install%" == "1" (
if "%Uninstall%" == "1" (
goto LHelp
)
)

if "%Install%" == "" (
if "%Uninstall%" == "" (
set Install=1
```

```
)
)

if "%TargetSiteUrl%" == "" (
if "%TargetWebUrl%" == "" (
set TargetWebUrl=%DefaultWebUrl%
set TargetSiteUrl=%DefaultSiteUrl%
)
if not "%TargetWebUrl%" == "" (
set TargetSiteUrl=%TargetWebUrl%
echo Setting TargetSiteUrl to be %TargetWebUrl%
)
)

if "%TargetWebUrl%" == "" (
set TargetWebUrl=%TargetSiteUrl%
echo Setting TargetWebUrl to be %TargetSiteUrl%
)

goto LMain

@rem--------------------------------------------------------------
@rem LHelp
@rem--------------------------------------------------------------
:LHelp
echo Usage:
echo setup.bat [/install or /uninstall][/weburl ^<url^>][/siteurl ^<url^>]
echo [/help]
echo.
echo Options:
echo /install or /uninstall
echo Install specified Solution package (.wsp) to the SharePoint server
echo or uninstall specified Solution from the SharePoint server.
echo Default value: install
echo /weburl
echo Specify a web url of the SharePoint server.
echo Default value: %DefaultWebUrl%
echo /siteurl
echo Specify a site url of the SharePoint server.
echo Default value: %DefaultSiteUrl%
```

296

```
echo /help
echo Show this information.
echo.

goto LTerminate

@rem----------------------------------------------------------------
@rem LMain
@rem----------------------------------------------------------------
:LMain
if "%Install%" == "1" (
call :LDeploy
)
if "%Uninstall%" == "1" (
call :LRetract
)

goto LTerminate

@rem----------------------------------------------------------------
@rem LDeploy
@rem----------------------------------------------------------------
:LDeploy
echo Adding solution %PackageName% to the SharePoint ...
"%SPAdminTool%" -o addsolution -filename "%PackageFile%"

echo Deploying solution %PackageName% ...
"%SPAdminTool%" -o deploysolution -name "%PackageName%" -local -
allowGacDeployment

echo Activating feature MyList ...
"%SPAdminTool%" -o activatefeature -id 06D1DF7A-3D3F-49b6-9388-74B8F26B50F2 -
url %TargetWebUrl%

goto :EOF


@rem----------------------------------------------------------------
@rem LRetract
@rem----------------------------------------------------------------
```

```
:LRetract
echo Deactivating feature MyList ...
"%SPAdminTool%" -o deactivatefeature -id 06D1DF7A-3D3F-49b6-9388-74B8F26B50F2
-url %TargetWebUrl%

echo Uninstalling feature MyList ...
"%SPAdminTool%" -o uninstallfeature -id 06D1DF7A-3D3F-49b6-9388-74B8F26B50F2 -
force

echo Retracting solution %PackageName% ...
"%SPAdminTool%" -o retractsolution -name "%PackageName%" -local

echo Deleting solution %PackageName% from SharePoint ...
"%SPAdminTool%" -o deletesolution -name "%PackageName%"

goto :EOF


@rem-----------------------------------------------------------------
@rem LTerminate
@rem-----------------------------------------------------------------
:LTerminate
set UserInput=
set /P UserInput=Hit enter key to quit.

set SPAdminTool=
set PackageFile=
set PackageName=
set Install=
set Uninstall=
set TargetSiteUrl=
set TargetWebUrl=
set UserInput=

popd
endlocal
```

Listing 7.51: *setup.bat*

298

Use Ctrl-H to replace all instances of "MyList" with your list's name. Also, don't forget to change the feature ID. ActivateFeature, DeactivateFeature and UninstallFeature commands should have your list's feature ID.

19. Compile the project.

20. Open command prompt and go to the project folder and run following command to create the WSP file:

```
makecab /f solution/cab.ddf
```

Listing 7.52: *Create solution file*

For example, If your project location is "C:\Projects\MyList", go to this folder and run the above command from the command prompt.

It will create a WSP for your list definition that you will be able to use to install or uninstall the list on other servers.

Download Visual Studio project (Project has all files needed to create the WSP):

http://walisystems.com/articles/SPS/Creating_list_definition/demo%20list%20gen%201.zip

Creating SharePoint list view dynamically

Here is another interesting topic. Interesting, for the people who are stuck and trying hard to achieve the objective. May be boring, for those who are working on something, who were never asked by their bosses to play with SharePoint "Views". I created this solution because, I myself, got stuck once. Let me explain the problem. The problem (requirement) was to filter the view dynamically. What? That's easy! I knew you would say that. Filters can only be applied on a single field or a field that contains a text value. If I ask you to filter a view based on a column "Country", this column is a promoted column. It was promoted from an InfoPath form. The column itself was a repeating table inside the InfoPath form. If you know what I am talking about, then you know that repeating tables cannot be promoted as a field in SharePoint. I promoted the repeating table as a comma separated single value. Again the problem remains there because filter cannot be applied on a field or column that has comma or a dot or whatever. I know it's confusing. Let me give you an example. There is a SharePoint library called "Lib A" that has a column called "Country". It has two values, in fact, one value separated by a comma. The value is "USA". I am in another SharePoint site that has a link. The link simply points to the "Lib A" library. The link opens a filtered view of the library "Lib A". How do you do that? This is a separate question but I will give the answer here. You pass the filter in the URL. Because you are applying a filter dynamically, you will create the link to open the library "Lib A" dynamically also. Here is the code:

```
string link =
"http://server/User%20Registration/Forms/AllItems.aspx?SourceType=Country=&FilterField1={"
+ filter + "}&FilterValue1=USA");
```

Listing 7.53: *Create link*

"SourceType=" is "Country" field. "FilterField1" is a GUID value of "Country" field. "FilterValue1" is the value that will be searched upon. We have passed "USA" as the parameter to this variable. This link will open a filtered view of the library and only items that have country as "USA" will be shown. So the question is from where do we get the GUID of the "Country" column. Here is the code to get the GUID:

```
SPSite site = SPContext.Current.Site;
SPWeb web = site.OpenWeb();

SPList list = web.Lists["Conntries"];

SPFieldCollection fldCollection = list.Fields;

string filter = Convert.ToString(fldCollection["Country"].Id);
```

Listing 7.54: *Get GUID*

This link will show you a filtered view. Let's get back to the original problem. This approach worked because the Country contained a single value, something like USA or UK or Mexico but the approach would fail if the field had a value like "USA, UK, Mexico" The filter won't work in that scenario and the approach would fail. So the solution to this problem is to create a filtered view dynamically and clicking the link will open the newly created view. Note the difference in the two approaches. The first one is not creating a new view. It's applying a filter on an already created view. The second approach creates a filtered view dynamically and then opens that view. The second approach helps for the scenarios where a field has multiple values. As I said, I had a requirement once which involved promoting a repeating table and applying filter on that. The second approach gave me a perfect solution. The code to create the filtered view is as following:

```
SPSite site = SPContext.Current.Site;
SPWeb web = site.OpenWeb();

SPList list = web.Lists["Countries"];

string CountryName = "USA";

SPViewCollection oViewCollection = list.Views;

int iExistingViews = list.Views.Count + 1;

string strViewName = "FilteredView" + iExistingViews;

System.Collections.Specialized.StringCollection viewFields =
```

```
new System.Collections.Specialized.StringCollection();

viewFields.Add("Type");
viewFields.Add("First Name");
viewFields.Add("Last Name");
viewFields.Add("Address");
viewFields.Add("Zip");
viewFields.Add("City");
viewFields.Add("State");
viewFields.Add("Country");
viewFields.Add("Phone");
viewFields.Add("Fax");
viewFields.Add("Web");

string query = "<Where><Contains><FieldRef Name=\"Country\"/>" +

"<Value Type=\"Text\">" + CountryName + "</Value></Contains></Where>";

oViewCollection.Add(strViewName, viewFields, query, 100, true, false);

web.Update();

string link = web.Url + "/" + list.Title + "/Forms/" + strViewName + ".aspx
```

Listing 7.55: *Create filtered view*

That's it. This code will generate a link that will open the newly created view with a list of filtered items. The code is simple and self explaining. I will explain the logic briefly. "iExistingViews" contains the count of existing view in the library. We increment it by 1 and use it to give a name to our new view. So if you decide to name the view as "FilteredView", you can append the count + 1 to give the view a unique name. This is to make sure that view is not created with the name that already exists. So we append "FilteredView" with the count of existing views plus 1. If existing count is 2, the new name will be "FilteredView3". It's up to you which fields you want to show in the view. I included all the fields of the "user registration" library. "CountryName" variable contains "USA" (for testing). The following line adds the view:

```
oViewCollection.Add(strViewName, viewFields, query, 100, true, false);
```

Listing 7.56: *Add view to views collection*

The fourth parameter in the above function represents the number of items to show in the view. The link that is created in the end will open the filtered view of the library.

Summary

This chapter acquainted you with different programming approaches. It has lots of code examples that you can learn from. Creating a web service to be consumed in SharePoint is a very interesting as well as popular topic. This chapter not only gave you code for the web service but also taught you about the intricacies of deploying the web service. It taught you how to create an installer in .NET to deploy your custom built web service with ease, using a wizard. This chapter also gave you web part examples. Code was explained along with the functionality offered by the code. Last two sections are about creating list definition and list view. Both these topics are important. If you were a developer, you would have enjoyed these sections the most. Creating list and site definitions is an important part of SharePoint development life cycle. In this chapter, we discussed creating list definition. We also saw how to create a Windows solution package for the SharePoint list. SharePoint views offer a way to see data in different ways. Views created in SharePoint can consist of different sets of fields and can be filtered or not filtered. In this chapter, you saw how you can create these views programmatically.

Chapter 8

Some Useful Tips

In this chapter:

- Fix "Operation is not valid due to the current state of the object" error
- Fix "A deployment or retraction is already under way for the solution …" error
- Fix "Null is null or not an object" error
- Button's event doesn't fire
- Value does not fall within the expected range
- Fix "Invalid column name C2" error
- Using caspol.exe to add assemblies to full trust assembly list
- Fix "Calling GetScopeID from a non-Office server binary" error
- Fix "Could not find the installable ISAM" error
- Using AND in SPQuery
- What is the data type of Yes/No field in SharePoint?
- Setting expiration date in a content type policy

SharePoint is a huge product. You can be a good expert of SharePoint but still cannot master all areas of this product. Developers usually scream about small issues that hinder their development efforts. One reason for this I see is lack of development support for SharePoint in Visual Studio. Visual Studio 2005 extensions provided good support for development but still lacked the punch. Well, no more worries! Visual Studio 2010 has very good inbuilt support for SharePoint development. Upcoming version of SharePoint, SharePoint 2010, will be well integrated with Visual Studio 2010 and development will not be as difficult as it is now. This chapter will show some tips and this will give you an idea of what kind of problems you can face in SharePoint. These are only a handful of tips. There are hundreds of tips available online on user blogs. A whole book can be devoted to the SharePoint tips. Although, this book covered several key sections and each chapter and section gave you a tip or trick but a whole book just covering tips is still a very good idea. I hope you will find the tips given in this chapter useful.

Tip 1: Fix "Operation is not valid due to the current state of the object" error

This is one of the common errors that you see during SharePoint development. There could be many reasons for this error to occur. Here I will discuss one scenario. I have noticed that sometimes calling SPContext throws this error. It seems to be a bug. The code works for the first time but throws an error if you run the same statement again (during the same session). For example, consider the following code:

```
SPSecurity.RunWithElevatedPrivileges(
delegate()
{
    using (SPSite site = new SPSite(SPContext.Current.Site.ID))
    using (SPWeb web = site.OpenWeb(SPContext.Current.Web.ID))

    string ItemID = web.Lists["myList"].Items[0]["ItemID"].ToString();
}
);
```

Listing 8.1: *Run with elevated privileges*

Interestingly, sometimes this code works but sometimes it fails after running successfully for the first time. I feel something goes wrong with the session. SPContext returns correct context when accessed for the first time but then throws the following error:

Operation is not valid due to the current state of the object

The error goes away if you remove the SPContext code and hard code the site and web values, for example:

```
SPSecurity.RunWithElevatedPrivileges(
delegate()
{
```

306

```
    using (SPSite site = new SPSite(http://server/))
    using (SPWeb web = site.OpenWeb("myweb"))

    string ItemID = web.Lists["myList"].Items[0]["ItemID"].ToString();


}


);
```

Listing 8.2: *Run with elevated privileges using hardcoded value*s

Obviously, we can not hard code the values in professional level applications. So, what's the solution? How can we get rid of this error? The error can be avoided if we write the same code in a different way. Here is the modified code:

```
SPWeb  webContext = null; //declare webContext out side the try ... catch and assign "null"

try
{

    webContext = SPContext.Current.Web; // Assign SPContext to the webContext

    SPSecurity.RunWithElevatedPrivileges(
    delegate()
    {
        using (SPSite site = new SPSite(webContext.Site.ID))
        using (SPWeb web = site.OpenWeb(webContext.ID))

        string ItemID = web.Lists["myList"].Items[0]["ItemID"].ToString();
    }
);

}

catch (Exception ex)
{
```

```
}

finally
{
    if (webContext != null)
        webContext.Dispose();
}
```

Listing 8.4: *Correct way of using elevated privileges*

Now, you won't get any error. Note that we declared the webContext outside the try... catch block and used SPContext only once. You can get "site" by calling webContext.Site.ID and similarly you can get "web" by calling webContext.ID. It's important that you dispose off the object after using it.

Tip 2: Fix "A deployment or retraction is already under way for the solution ..." error

You get this error when you try to publish an already published InfoPath form in SharePoint:

A deployment or retraction is already under way for the solution ...

If you go into the event log, you will notice different error messages related to this event. For example, one message will be as following:

EventType ulsexception12, P1 w3wp.exe, P2 6.0.3790.1830, P3 42435be1, P4 microsoft.office.infopath.server, P5 12.0.4518.0, P6 4541816a, P7 12961, P8 161, P9 nullreferenceexception, P10 8gec.

Another will look like the following:

An exception occurred during loading of business logic. (User: Server\Administrator, Form Name: Teachers, IP: , Request: http://Server/_layouts/Formserver.aspx?XsnLocation=http://server/FormServerTemplates/teach ers.xsn, Type: FileNotFoundException, Exception Message: Could not load file or assembly 'file:///C:\Program Files\Common Files\Microsoft Shared\Web Server Extensions\12\Template\Features\FT-01-08f7ce0d-e5ba-7eab-8b14-ac2eb94f1add\Teachers.dll' or one of its dependencies. The system cannot find the file specified.)

For more information, see Help and Support Center

Now both these messages are misleading. The first one shows a "nullreferenceexception" and the other one mentions a missing file or dependency. Because of these messages one tends to waste time in trying to resolve the "nullreferenceexception" error. The error occurs if somehow the form didn't get published properly the first time it is published in SharePoint. During our experiments, on each attempt SharePoint threw a new error message. One thing that I noticed was that the publishing process stopped the "Windows SharePoint Services Administration" service which was one of the reasons we were unable to republish the form. So check services and start this service if it's stopped and then run the following command:

```
stsadm -o execadmsvcjobs
```

Listing 8.5: *Run stsadm command*

If you try to publish the form without starting the "Windows SharePoint Services Administration" service, you will get the following error:

"The timer job for the operation has been created. However, it cannot be run because the administrative service for this server is not enabled."

So start the service and run the stsadm command. This will publish your form and hopefully, you will get rid of the error that said that there was a "nullreferenceexception" in your form. If you still get the same error (A deployment or retraction is already ...) then try running the following command to cancel the deployment that was started earlier:

```
stsadm –o canceldeployment –id <Timer Job ID>
```

Listing 8.6: *Cancel deployment using stsadm command*

Timer Job ID can be copied from "Central Administration > Operations > Timer Job Definitions" page. See the most recently created job, you can also verify by looking at the title. Right click the "Job" link and copy the URL. Locate the "JobId" parameter in the URL, this parameter contains the ID.

Tip 3: Fix "Null is null or not an object" error

Have you seen this error before? Did you find a solution? I was getting this javascript error on the click of a button that had a simple rule attached to it. Everytime I clicked the button, it produced this javascript error:

Null is null or not an object.

After some debugging, I noticed that the error was occuring in the "owsbrows.js". This file contained a line that was trying to load a value from the control that was clicked in the form. The control returned "null" and hence InfoPath generated this beautiful error message.

Reason?

The postback setting of the button was set to "Never".

Solution?

Set the postback setting of the button to "Always".

1. Right click the button.
2. Select "Button Properties".
3. Select "Browser forms" tab.
4. Select "Always". Note: Selecting the default recommended option "Only when necessary for correct rendering of the form (recommended)"will not solve this problem.

When you are using rules, you must set the postback settings of the button to "Always" so that the click event sends data to the server everytime the button is clicked.

Tip 4: Button's event doesn't fire

I had a button in my form and there was a simple rule attached to this button. Rule was that If someone clicked the button, a (hidden) textbox would appear in the form, a very simple rule! Problem?? The button was not working. Somehow the event was not firing. I had this problem even before but simply changing the ID of the button resolved my problem but this time, changing the ID didn't work. I spent a couple of hours trying to find the cause but in the end, I needed a quick solution as I was short of time (as usual). The problem was resolved when I added an empty event handler for the button in the form.

```
((ButtonEvent)EventManager.ControlEvents["Button"]).Clicked += new
ClickedEventHandler(Button_Clicked);

 public void Button_Clicked(object sender, ClickedEventArgs e)
 {
     // Write your code here.
 }
```

Listing 8.7: *Button_Clicked() event*

It's still a mystery to me why some buttons work without an event handler and the others don't. I added two buttons to the form, one was firing the other was not! This simple tip may come in handy for some of you reading this.

Tip 5: Value does not fall within the expected range

When working on large applications, we usually make mistakes and then spend time debugging the errors that occur because of the mistakes that we make during programming but there are some errors that occur even if you don't make any mistake. Have a look at the following code:

```
SPWeb web = Site.OpenWeb(SPContext.Current.Web.ID);
string strList = SPContext.Current.Web.Url.Substring( .... substring processing ....);
SPList list = web.Lists[strList]; //This line gives error!
```

Listing 8.8: *Accessing list programmatically*

Do you see any problem with this code? I didn't notice any thing. It gave me the following error:

*Value does not fall within the expected range.
Source: Microsoft.SharePoint
Stack trace: at Microsoft.SharePoint.SPListCollection.GetListByName(String strListName, Boolean bThrowException)*

at Microsoft.SharePoint.SPListCollection.get_Item(String strListName)

The reason of the error turned out to be the list name. The list name had parentheses which resulted in the error. In small companies, you are the all in all when working on a project but in big companies or when working on large projects, there are several people involved in the project. The list was created by the SharePoint admin and I was getting the list name programmatically. I didn't know the list name had parentheses in it. When you load such a list in browser, SharePoint automatically removes parentheses from the list name and the list works fine but when you try to access the same list programmatically, SharePoint gives you an error. As you will notice, in the code above, I am extracting the list name from "SPContext.Current.Web.Url" and It returns the list name without parentheses in it while the actual list name has parentheses and hence you get an error. Even if you add parentheses to the list name (in your code), you still get an error but a different one. It's a **SPException** error and returns following message:

Action can not be completed.

Conclusion: Do not use parentheses in list name.

Tip 6: Fix "Invalid column name C2" error

SharePoint gives you this error when you try to search documents using the SPQuery object and you search by passing the document's Name. SPQuery object uses the internal field names so it's important to pass correct internal name for the correct field to be searched. By default, the "Name" field that is visible in the library has the internal name "LinkFilename" so when someone wants to search a document in the library using the "Name" field, obviously he uses the "LinkFilename" to search the document but strangely enough, it returns the following error:

Invalid column name C2

This error occurs in the SQL Server. SharePoint tries to search this field in the DB and returns an error when the field is not found. I haven't checked whether this field actually exists in the DB or not but we get an error. There are two more "Name" fields in the library. The internal names of the three "Name" fields are as following:

Name="**LinkFilename**" DisplayName="Name FieldType="Computed" *-> default*

Name="**FileLeafRef**" DisplayName="Name" FieldType="File"

Name="**LinkFilenameNoMenu**" DisplayName="Name" FieldType="Computed"

If you look at the definitions, you will notice that the FieldType of the two fields is "Computed" and for one field, it is "File". By default, it is the first field that is shown in the library. It has the FieldType "Computed". To search the document in the library using the "Name" field, you must use the second field that has the internal name "FileLeafRef". Although, this field is not visible in the library by default but it will return the document in the search. It's FieldType is "File" and therefore, you will have to pass the complete filename alongwith the extension in order for search to work and return the document. The third "Name" field also errors out. It is not necessary to make this field visible in the library to make the search work.

```
SPQuery query = new SPQuery();
query.Query = "<Where><Eq><FieldRef Name='FileLeafRef'></FieldRef><Value
Type='Text'>" + itemName + "</Value></Eq></Where>";

SPListItemCollection listitems = list.GetItems(query);
```

Listing 8.9: *Sample query*

"itemName" is the parameter that contains the file's name (passed from the interface or the calling function). It will be the complete name (alongwith extension), for example, document1.doc.

Tip 7: Using caspol.exe to add assemblies to full trust assembly list

Code Access Security Policy Tool (Caspol.exe) can be used to modify security policy for different policy levels. You can use it to add an assembly to the full trust assembly list for a specific policy level. Security exception is common when you try to run your application from a network share. See following article for more details:

http://blogs.msdn.com/shawnfa/archive/2003/06/20/57023.aspx

You also get stuck sometimes when you try to deploy your application to a local folder. See following article for details:

http://blogs.msdn.com/vsto2/archive/2005/10/12/480130.aspx

In this tip, I will show you how you can use caspol.exe to add your assembly to a full trust assembly list.

caspol.exe is located in the following directory:

LocalDrive:\Windows\Microsoft.Net\Framework\v2.0.50727\

Use the following command to put an assembly to the trust:

```
caspol.exe -u -addgroup All_Code -url "\*"  FullTrust -name "Your Assembly Name"
```

Listing 8.10: *caspol.exe*

Assembly name will be like "YourCompany.ApplicationName" (without extension)

Suppose, you are deploying your application on a remote machine using a script. How will you run the caspol.exe tool on the remote machine? One way is to create a batch file and run it programmatically on the remote machine after copying the assembly to that machine. Create a batch file and copy the following in the file:

316

```
CD \
PATH=%windir%\microsoft.net\framework\v2.0.50727\
caspol.exe -polchgprompt off -u -addgroup All_Code -url "\*"  FullTrust -name
"MyAssembly"
caspol.exe -polchgprompt on
```

Listing 8.11: *Batch file to run caspol.exe*

polchgprompt option enables or disables the prompt that is displayed whenever Caspol.exe is run using an option that would cause policy changes. **addgroup** adds a new code group to the code group hierarchy. For more details, see following article:

http://msdn2.microsoft.com/en-us/library/cb6t8dtz.aspx

Now, call this batch file programmatically from your deployment application.

```
string tempFolder = Environment.GetEnvironmentVariable("Temp");

FileStream fyle = new FileStream(tempFolder +
"file://errlog.txt",FileMode.Create,FileAccess.Write/);
StreamWriter sw = new StreamWriter(fyle);
sw.Write("Ready to run the batch file!");

System.Diagnostics.Process proc = new System.Diagnostics.Process();
proc.EnableRaisingEvents = false;
proc.StartInfo.FileName = Environment.CurrentDirectory + "\\security.bat";

proc.Start();
sw.Write("security.bat ran successfully!");
sw.Close();
```

Listing 8.12: *Call batch file programmatically*

Remember, this can be an unattended installation, so you may want to log errors. You can log errors to the Windows log file. You can also create your own text file for logging errors, as shown in the code above. The code creates "errlog.txt" file in the Windows' Temp directory and

317

then executes the batch file. This code does not show how to trap and log errors, you can simply use try ... catch blocks to write the errors in the text file.

Using this technique you can put assemblies to a list of full trust assemblies.

Tip 8: Fix "Calling GetScopeID from a non-Office server binary" error

Scopes are usually used in search code. One of the very common errors when working with scopes in search code is as following:

"Calling GetScopeID from a non-Office server binary."

This error occurs when you instantiate the query object, for example:

```
KeywordQuery kwQuery = new KeywordQuery(site);
```

Listing 8.13: *keywordquery*

To resolve this issue, include the correct namespace when defining the **kwQuery** object, for example:

```
Microsoft.Office.Server.Search.Query.KeywordQuery kwQuery = new
Microsoft.Office.Server.Search.Query.KeywordQuery(site)
```

Listing 8.14: *Using correct search object*

When you skip the namespace, SharePoint tries to call the GetScopeID() from an assembly different than the one it should be using. This especially happens when both of the following namespaces are included in your code:

```
using Microsoft.SharePoint.Search.Query;
using Microsoft.Office.Server;
```

Listing 8.15: *Conflicting namespaces*

Tip 9: Fix "Could not find the installable ISAM" error

Small tip!! Some times things so small take up so much of your precious time that you start getting frustrated. The following is a common error people get when trying to connect with an Excel or Access DB using the Oledb:

Could not find the installable ISAM.

I agree there could be many reasons for this error to occur. For example, the drivers on your system are corrupted, in that case, you will have to reinstall the drivers or may the registry entries are corrupted. For that you will have to modify the registry. (If that is the case, you may want to look at the MS knowledge base article (http://support.microsoft.com/kb/209805) that provides the solution). One scenario in which you could get this error is, if you are using Office 2007 and you are try to connect to an Excel file using following connection string:

```
string excelConnectionString = @"Provider=Microsoft.Jet.OLEDB.4.0;Data
Source=C:\Temp\metadata.xls;Extended Properties=Excel 12.0";
```

Listing 8.16: *Excel connection string*

Can you locate the problem in the connection string? Give it a try! The string is syntactically correct then where is the problem? The problem is with the "Extended Properties". If I replace "Excel 12.0" with "Excel 8.0" (which is the correct version actually), the problem goes away. I was about to modify my registry when luckily I noticed the correct version and modified my connection string and everything started working fine.

The error message that one gets is so generic that anyone will be easily deluded and this wastes time.

Tip 10: Using AND in SPQuery

Ok, here is a small tip for the beginners. If you are trying to search records based on two values, for example, "select * from list where a=1 and b=2" then how will you write its equivalent using the SPQuery object. Here is the sample:

```
SPQuery query = new SPQuery();
query.Query = "<Where><And><Eq><FieldRef Name='Field1'></FieldRef><Value
Type='Number'>1</Value></Eq><Gt><FieldRef Name='Field2'></FieldRef><Value
Type='Number'>0</Value></Gt></And></Where>";
```

Listing 8.17: *SPQuery*

This query will find records where Field1 = 1 and Field2 > 0.

So you have learnt two new things, using "And" and "Gt".

Tip 11: What is the data type of Yes/No field in SharePoint?

Value type has to be provided when writing a query for the SPQuery object. How do you access a Yes/No field or let's put it in another way! What is the data type of the Yes/No field in SharePoint? The data type is "Boolean" and the value has to be provided as 1 or 0. Providing a value of Yes or No or True or False will not work. Ok, sometimes the query fails even if you provided the value as 1 or 0. You get a strange error. Following is the error message:

One or more field types are not installed properly. Go to the list settings page to delete these fields

To fix this error, you will have to use the internal name of the field in the spquery. Yes, internal names can be different from the names displayed in the site. For example, internal name for the field "My Field" can be "My_x0020_Field".

Here is the sample code:

```
SPQuery query = new SPQuery();
query.Query = "<Where><Eq>FieldRef Name='My_x0020_Field'></FieldRef><Value
Type='Boolean'>1</Value></Eq></Where>";
```

Listing 8.18: *SPQuery*

This will search for records where "My Field" has the value of 1 (Yes).

Easiest way to find the internal name of the field is to open the "New" form in browser and then view it's source. Right-click any where in the "New" form to open the context menu and select "View Source". You will find the fields along with their internal names near the end of the source file.

Tip 12: Setting expiration date in a content type policy

1. This will work if you have SharePoint Standard or Enterprise edition. Open your site in a browser.

2. Select "Site Actions > Site Settings".

3. Click "Go to top level site settings". Of course, you don't see this link if you are already on the top level site.

4. Click "Site content types" under "Galleries".

5. Locate the content type that you want to use for setting the policy on. Click the link of the content type.

6. Click "Information management policy settings" under "Settings".

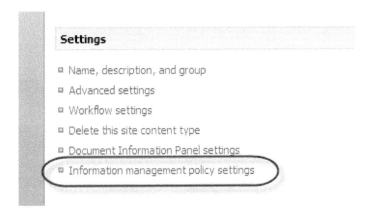

Figure 8.1: *Settings*

7. Select "Define a policy..." option and click OK.

Figure 8.2: *Define a policy*

8. Check "Enable Expiration" checkbox. Select "Created" or "Modified" in the item's properties and select days, months or years from the last drop down in the row. Enter a number in the middle text box. Now select action. You can choose the default action "Delete" or you can start a workflow and do custom actions. Click OK to save the settings.

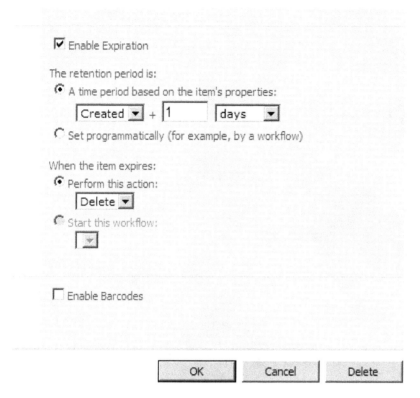

Figure 8.3: *Setting Expiration*

Hope this will help someone. It is straight forward but I have seen users asking this question "How to set expiration policy on a content type".

Summary

This chapter was a collection of tips. Even when you have mastered something, it is not impossible to get trapped in issues that seemed trivial but took extensive time to resolve. These small tips come in handy in the situations when the major task had been accomplished but one small minor issue delayed the final roll out of the application. There are hundreds of tips that are shared by the developers and bloggers on their sites and blogs and are of immense importance and offer great help to the developer and user community. This chapter offered some of the tips just to give you the flavor of what types of problems you can encounter in SharePoint and what kind of tips and tricks you can use to resolve these issues.

Index

www.ingramcontent.com/pod-product-compliance
Lightning Source LLC
Chambersburg PA
CBHW062056050326
40690CB00016B/3113